Minnesota Twins 2021

A Baseball Companion

Edited by Steven Goldman and Bret Sayre

Baseball Prospectus

Craig Brown, Associate Editor
Robert Au, Harry Pavlidis and Amy Pircher, Statistics Editors

Copyright © 2021 by DIY Baseball, LLC.
All rights reserved

This book or any part thereof may not be reproduced or transmitted in any form or by any means, electronic or mechanical, including photocopying, recording, or by any information storage and retrieval system, without permission in writing from the publisher.

Limit of Liability/Disclaimer of Warranty: While the publisher and the author have used their best efforts in preparing this book, they make no representations or warranties with respect to the accuracy or completeness of the contents of this book and specifically disclaim any implied warranties of merchantability or fitness for a particular purpose. No warranty may be created or extended by sales representatives or written sales materials. The advice and strategies contained herein may not be suitable for your situation. You should consult with a professional where appropriate. Neither the publisher nor the author shall be liable for any loss of profit or any other commercial damages, including but not limited to special, incidental, consequential, or other damages.

Library of Congress Cataloging-in-Publication Data:
paperback
ISBN-13: 978-1-950716-57-9

Project Credits
Cover Design: Ginny Searle
Interior Design and Production: Amy Pircher, Robert Au
Layout: Amy Pircher, Robert Au

Baseball icon courtesy of Uberux, from https://www.shareicon.net/author/uberux

Ballpark diagram courtesy of Lou Spirito/THIRTY81 Project, https://thirty81project.com/

Manufactured in the United States of America
10 9 8 7 6 5 4 3 2 1

Table of Contents

Statistical Introduction v

Part 1: Team Analysis
Performance Graphs 3
2020 Team Performance 4
2021 Team Projections 5
Team Personnel 6
Target Field Stats 7
Twins Team Analysis 9

Part 2: Player Analysis
Twins Player Analysis 14
Twins Prospects 89

Part 3: Featured Articles
Twins All-Time Top 10 Players 103
    by Rob Mains

A Taxonomy of 2020 Abnormalities 109
    by Rob Mains

Tranches of WAR 115
    by Russell A. Carleton

Secondhand Sport 121
    by Patrick Dubuque

Steve Dalkowski Dreaming 125
    by Steven Goldman

A Reward For A Functioning Society 129
    by Cory Frontin and Craig Goldstein

Index of Names 133

Statistical Introduction

Sports are, fundamentally, a blend of athletic endeavor and storytelling. Baseball, like any other sport, tells its stories in so many ways: in the arc of a game from the stands or a season from the box scores, in photos, or even in numbers. At Baseball Prospectus, we understand that statistics don't replace observation or any of baseball's stories, but complement everything else that makes the game so much fun.

What stats help us with is with patterns and precision, variance and value. This book can help you learn things you may not see from watching a game or hundred, whether it's the path of a career over time or the breadth of the entire MLB. We'd also never ask you to choose between our numbers and the experience of viewing a game from the cheap seats or the comfort of your home; our publication combines running the numbers with observations and wisdom from some of the brightest minds we can find. But if you *do* want to learn more about the numbers beyond what's on the backs of player jerseys, let us help explain.

Offense

We've revised our methodology for determining batting value. Long-time readers of the book will notice that we've retired True Average in favor of a new metric: Deserved Runs Created Plus (DRC+). Developed by Jonathan Judge and our stats team, this statistic measures everything a player does at the plate–reaching base, hitting for power, making outs, and moving runners over–and puts it on a scale where 100 equals league-average performance. A DRC+ of 150 is terrific, a DRC+ of 100 is average and a DRC+ of 75 means you better be an excellent defender.

DRC+ also does a better job than any of our previous metrics in taking contextual factors into account. The model adjusts for how the park affects performance, but also for things like the talent of the opposing pitcher, value of different types of batted-ball events, league, temperature and other factors. It's able to describe a player's expected offensive contribution than any other statistic we've found over the years, and also does a better job of predicting future performance as well.

Minnesota Twins 2021

The other aspect of run-scoring is baserunning, which we quantify using Baserunning Runs. BRR not only records the value of stolen bases (or getting caught in the act), but also accounts for all the stuff that doesn't show up on the back of a baseball card: a runner's ability to go first to third on a single, or advance on a fly ball.

Defense

Where offensive value is *relatively* easy to identify and understand, defensive value is … not. Over the past dozen years, the sabermetric community has focused mostly on stats based on zone data: a real-live human person records the type of batted ball and estimated landing location, and models are created that give expected outs. From there, you can compare fielders' actual outs to those expected ones. Simple, right?

Unfortunately, zone data has two major issues. First, zone data is recorded by commercial data providers who keep the raw data private unless you pay for it. (All the statistics we build in this book and on our website use public data as inputs.) That hurts our ability to test assumptions or duplicate results. Second, over the years it has become apparent that there's quite a bit of "noise" in zone-based fielding analysis. Sometimes the conclusions drawn from zone data don't hold up to scrutiny, and sometimes the different data provided by different providers don't look anything alike, giving wildly different results. Sometimes the hard-working professional stringers or scorers might unknowingly inflict unconscious bias into the mix: for example good fielders will often be credited with more expected outs despite the data, and ballparks with high press boxes tend to score more line drives than ones with a lower press box.

Enter our Fielding Runs Above Average (FRAA). For most positions, FRAA is built from play-by-play data, which allows us to avoid the subjectivity found in many other fielding metrics. The idea is this: count how many fielding plays are made by a given player and compare that to expected plays for an average fielder at their position (based on pitcher ground ball tendencies and batter handedness). Then we adjust for park and base-out situations.

When it comes to catchers, our methodology is a little different thanks to the laundry list of responsibilities they're tasked with beyond just, well, catching and throwing the ball. By now you've probably heard about "framing" or the art of making umpires more likely to call balls outside the strike zone for strikes. To put this into one tidy number, we incorporate pitch tracking data (for the years it exists) and adjust for important factors like pitcher, umpire, batter and home-field advantage using a mixed-model approach. This grants us a number for how many strikes the catcher is personally adding to (or subtracting from) his pitchers' performance … which we then convert to runs added or lost using linear weights.

Framing is one of the biggest parts of determining catcher value, but we also take into account blocking balls from going past, whether a scorer deems it a passed ball or a wild pitch. We use a similar approach—one that really benefits from the pitch tracking data that tells us what ends up in the dirt and what doesn't. We also include a catcher's ability to prevent stolen bases and how well they field balls in play, and *finally* we come up with our FRAA for catchers.

Pitching

Both pitching and fielding make up the half of baseball that isn't run scoring: run prevention. Separating pitching from fielding is a tough task, and most recent pitching analysis has branched off from Voros McCracken's famous (and controversial) statement, "There is little if any difference among major-league pitchers in their ability to prevent hits on balls hit in the field of play." The research of the analytic community has validated this to some extent, and there are a host of "defense-independent" pitching measures that have been developed to try and extract the effect of the defense behind a hurler from the pitcher's work.

Our solution to this quandary is Deserved Run Average (DRA), our core pitching metric. DRA seeks to evaluate a pitcher's performance, much like earned run average (ERA), the tried-and-true pitching stat you've seen on every baseball broadcast or box score from the past century, but it's very different. To start, DRA takes an event-by-event look at what the pitchers does, and adjusts the value of that event based on different environmental factors like park, batter, catcher, umpire, base-out situation, run differential, inning, defense, home field advantage, pitcher role and temperature. That mixed model gives us a pitcher's expected contribution, similar to what we do for our DRC+ model for hitters and FRAA model for catchers. (Oh, and we also consider the pitcher's effect on basestealing and on balls getting past the catcher.)

DRA is set to the scale of runs allowed per nine innings (RA9) instead of ERA, which makes DRA's scale slightly higher than ERA's. Because of this, for ease of use, we're supplying DRA-, which is much easier for the reader to parse. As with DRC+, DRA- is an "index" stat, meaning instead of using some arbitrary and shifting number to denote what's "good," average is always 100. The reason that it uses a minus rather than a plus is because like ERA, a lower number is better. Therefore a 75 DRA- describes a performance 25 percent better than average, whereas a 150 DRA- means that either a pitcher is getting extremely lucky with their results, or getting ready to try a new pitch.

Since the last time you picked up an edition of this book, we've also made a few minor changes to DRA to make it better. Recent research into "tunneling"—the act of throwing consecutive pitches that appear similar from a batter's point of view until after the swing decision point–data has given us a new contextual factor to account for in DRA: plate distance. This refers to the distance between successive pitches as they approach the plate, and while it has a smaller effect than factors like velocity or whiff rate, it still can help explain pitcher strikeout rate in our model.

Recently Added Descriptive Statistics

Returning to our 2021 edition of the book are a few figures which recently appeared. These numbers may be a little bit more familiar to those of you who have spent some time investigating baseball statistics.

Fastball Percentage

Our fastball percentage (FA%) statistic measures how frequently a pitcher throws a pitch classified as a "fastball," measured as a percentage of overall pitches thrown. We qualify three types of fastballs:

1. The traditional four-seam fastball;
2. The two-seam fastball or sinker;
3. "Hard cutters," which are pitches that have the movement profile of a cut fastball and are used as the pitcher's primary offering or in place of a more traditional fastball.

For example, a pitcher with a FA% of 67 throws any combination of these three pitches about two-thirds of the time.

Whiff Rate

Everybody loves a swing and a miss, and whiff rate (Whiff%) measures how frequently pitchers induce a swinging strike. To calculate Whiff%, we add up all the pitches thrown that ended with a swinging strike, then divide that number by a pitcher's total pitches thrown. Most often, high whiff rates correlate with high strikeout rates (and overall effective pitcher performance).

Called Strike Probability

Called Strike Probability (CSP) is a number that represents the likelihood that all of a pitcher's pitches will be called a strike while controlling for location, pitcher and batter handedness, umpire and count. Here's how it works: on each pitch, our model determines how many times (out of 100) that a similar pitch was called for a strike given those factors mentioned above, and when normalized for each batter's strike zone. Then we average the CSP for all pitches thrown by a pitcher in a season, and that gives us the yearly CSP percentage you see in the stats boxes.

As you might imagine, pitchers with a higher CSP are more likely to work in the zone, where pitchers with a lower CSP are likely locating their pitches outside the normal strike zone, for better or for worse.

Projections

Many of you aren't turning to this book just for a look at what a player has done, but for a look at what a player is going to do: the PECOTA projections. PECOTA, initially developed by Nate Silver (who has moved on to greater fame as a political analyst), consists of three parts:

1. Major-league equivalencies, which use minor-league statistics to project how a player will perform in the major leagues;
2. Baseline forecasts, which use weighted averages and regression to the mean to estimate a player's current true talent level; and
3. Aging curves, which uses the career paths of comparable players to estimate how a player's statistics are likely to change over time.

With all those important things covered, let's take a look at what's in the book this year.

Team Prospectus

Most of this book is composed of team chapters, with one for each of the 30 major-league franchises. On the first page of each chapter, you'll see a box that contains some of the key statistics for each team as well as a very inviting stadium diagram.

We start with the team name, their unadjusted 2020 win-loss record, and their divisional ranking. Beneath that are a host of other team statistics. **Pythag** presents an adjusted 2020 winning percentage, calculated by taking runs scored per game (**RS/G**) and runs allowed per game (**RA/G**) for the team, and running them through a version of Bill James' Pythagorean formula that was refined and improved by David Smyth and Brandon Heipp. (The formula is called "Pythagenpat," which is equally fun to type and to say.)

Next up is **DRC+**, described earlier, to indicate the overall hitting ability of the team either above or below league-average. Run prevention on the pitching side is covered by **DRA** (also mentioned earlier) and another metric: Fielding Independent Pitching (**FIP**), which calculates another ERA-like statistic based on strikeouts, walks, and home runs recorded. Defensive Efficiency Rating (**DER**) tells us the percentage of balls in play turned into outs for the team, and is a quick fielding shorthand that rounds out run prevention.

After that, we have several measures related to roster composition, as opposed to on-field performance. **B-Age** and **P-Age** tell us the average age of a team's batters and pitchers, respectively. **Payroll** is the combined team payroll for all on-field players, and Doug Pappas' Marginal Dollars per Marginal Win (**M$/MW**) tells us how much money a team spent to earn production above replacement level.

Next to each of these stats, we've listed each team's MLB rank in that category from first to 30th. In this, first always indicates a positive outcome and 30th a negative outcome, except in the case of salary—first is highest.

After the franchise statistics, we share a few items about the team's home ballpark. There's the aforementioned diagram of the park's dimensions (including distances to the outfield wall), a graphic showing the height of the wall from the left-field pole to the right-field pole, and a table showing three-year park factors for the stadium. The park factors are displayed as indexes where 100 is average, 110 means that the park inflates the statistic in question by 10 percent, and 90 means that the park deflates the statistic in question by 10 percent.

On the second page of each team chapter, you'll find three graphs. The first is **Payroll History** and helps you see how the team's payroll has compared to the MLB and divisional average payrolls over time. Payroll figures are current as of January 1, 2021; with so many free agents still unsigned as of this writing, the final 2021 figure will likely be significantly different for many teams. (In the meantime, you can always find the most current data at Baseball Prospectus' Cot's Baseball Contracts page.)

The second graph is **Future Commitments** and helps you see the team's future outlays, if any.

The third graph is **Farm System Ranking** and displays how the Baseball Prospectus prospect team has ranked the organization's farm system since 2007.

After the graphs, we have a **Personnel** section that lists many of the important decision-makers and upper-level field and operations staff members for the franchise, as well as any former Baseball Prospectus staff members who are currently part of the organization. (In very rare circumstances, someone might be on both lists!)

Position Players

After all that information and a thoughtful bylined essay covering each team, we present our player comments. These are also bylined, but due to frequent franchise shifts during the offseason, our bylines are more a rough guide than a perfect accounting of who wrote what.

Each player is listed with the major-league team that employed him as of early January 2021. If a player changed teams after that point via free agency, trade, or any other method, you'll be able to find them in the chapter for their previous squad.

As an example, take a look at the player comment for Padres shortstop Fernando Tatis Jr.: the stat block that accompanies his written comment is at the top of this page. First we cover biographical information (age is as of June 30, 2021) before moving onto the stats themselves. Our statistic columns include standard identifying information like **YEAR**, **TEAM**, **LVL** (level of affiliated play) and **AGE** before getting into the numbers. Next, we provide raw, untranslated

Fernando Tatis Jr. SS
Born: 01/02/99   Age: 22   Bats: R   Throws: R
Height: 6'3"   Weight: 217   Origin: International Free Agent, 2015

YEAR	TEAM	LVL	AGE	PA	R	2B	3B	HR	RBI	BB	K	SB	CS	AVG/OBP/SLG
2018	SA	AA	19	394	77	22	4	16	43	33	109	16	5	.286/.355/.507
2019	SD	MLB	20	372	61	13	6	22	53	30	110	16	6	.317/.379/.590
2020	SD	MLB	21	257	50	11	2	17	45	27	61	11	3	.277/.366/.571
2021 FS	SD	MLB	22	600	95	24	4	31	81	50	165	17	8	.263/.331/.499
2021 DC	SD	MLB	22	628	100	25	4	32	85	53	173	19	8	.263/.331/.499

Comparables: Darryl Strawberry, Bo Bichette, Ronald Acuña Jr.

YEAR	TEAM	LVL	AGE	PA	DRC+	BABIP	BRR	FRAA	WARP
2018	SA	AA	19	394	136	.370	3.0	SS(83): -1.9	2.4
2019	SD	MLB	20	372	118	.410	7.1	SS(83): 0.9	3.4
2020	SD	MLB	21	257	126	.306	0.7	SS(57): -5.5	0.9
2021 FS	SD	MLB	22	600	126	.318	1.7	SS -1	3.9
2021 DC	SD	MLB	22	628	126	.318	1.8	SS -1	4.0

numbers like you might find on the back of your dad's baseball cards: **PA** (plate appearances), **R** (runs), **2B** (doubles), **3B** (triples), **HR** (home runs), **RBI** (runs batted in), **BB** (walks), **K** (strikeouts), **SB** (stolen bases) and **CS** (caught stealing).

Following the basic stats is **Whiff%** (whiff rate), which denotes how often, when a batter swings, he fails to make contact with the ball. Another way to think of this number is an inverse of a hitter's contact rate.

Next, we have unadjusted "slash" statistics: **AVG** (batting average), **OBP** (on-base percentage) and **SLG** (slugging percentage). Following the slash line is **DRC+** (Deserved Runs Created Plus), which we described earlier as total offensive expected contribution compared to the league average.

BABIP (batting average on balls in play) tells us how often a ball in play fell for a hit, and can help us identify whether a batter may have been lucky or not ... but note that high BABIPs also tend to follow the great hitters of our time, as well as speedy singles hitters who put the ball on the ground.

The next item is **BRR** (Baserunning Runs), which covers all of a player's baserunning accomplishments including (but not limited to) swiped bags and failed attempts. Next is **FRAA** (Fielding Runs Above Average), which also includes the number of games previously played at each position noted in parentheses. Multi-position players have only their two most frequent positions listed here, but their total FRAA number reflects all positions played.

Our last column here is **WARP** (Wins Above Replacement Player). WARP estimates the total value of a player, which means for hitters it takes into account hitting runs above average (calculated using the DRC+ model), BRR and FRAA. Then, it makes an adjustment for positions played and gives the player a credit for plate appearances based upon the difference between "replacement level"—which is derived from the quality of players added to a team's roster after the start of the season–and the league average.

The final line just below the stats box is **PECOTA** data, which is discussed further in a following section.

Catchers

Catchers are a special breed, and thus they have earned their own separate box which displays some of the defensive metrics that we've built just for them. As an example, let's check out Yasmani Grandal.

YEAR	TEAM	P. COUNT	FRM RUNS	BLK RUNS	THRW RUNS	TOT RUNS
2018	LAD	16816	15.7	0.8	0.1	16.5
2019	MIL	18740	19.4	1.8	-0.1	21.1
2020	CHW	4830	3.7	0.3	-0.2	3.8
2021	CHW	14430	16.7	-0.6	1.0	17.1
2021	CHW	14430	16.7	0.4	1.0	18.0

The **YEAR** and **TEAM** columns match what you'd find in the other stat box. **P. COUNT** indicates the number of pitches thrown while the catcher was behind the plate, including swinging strikes, fouls and balls in play. **FRM RUNS** is the total run value the catcher provided (or cost) his team by influencing the umpire to call strikes where other catchers did not. **BLK RUNS** expresses the total run value above or below average for the catcher's ability to prevent wild pitches and passed balls. **THRW RUNS** is calculated using a similar model as the previous two statistics, and it measures a catcher's ability to throw out basestealers but also to dissuade them from testing his arm in the first place. It takes into account factors like the pitcher (including his delivery and pickoff move) and baserunner (who could be as fast as Billy Hamilton or as slow as Yonder Alonso). **TOT RUNS** is the sum of all of the previous three statistics.

Pitchers

Let's give our pitchers a turn, using 2020 AL Cy Young winner Shane Bieber as our example. Take a look at his stat block: the first line and the **YEAR**, **TEAM**, **LVL** and **AGE** columns are the same as in the position player example earlier.

Here too, we have a series of columns that display raw, unadjusted statistics compiled by the pitcher over the course of a season: **W** (wins), **L** (losses), **SV** (saves), **G** (games pitched), **GS** (games started), **IP** (innings pitched), **H** (hits allowed) and **HR** (home runs allowed). Next we have two statistics that are rates: **BB/9** (walks per nine innings) and **K/9** (strikeouts per nine innings), before returning to the unadjusted K (strikeouts).

Next up is **GB%** (ground ball percentage), which is the percentage of all batted balls that were hit on the ground, including both outs and hits. Remember, this is based on observational data and subject to human error, so please approach this with a healthy dose of skepticism.

BABIP (batting average on balls in play) is calculated using the same methodology as it is for position players, but it often tells us more about a pitcher than it does a hitter. With pitchers, a high BABIP is often due to poor defense or bad luck, and can often be an indicator of potential rebound, and a low BABIP may be cause to expect performance regression. (A typical league-average BABIP is close to .290-.300.)

The metrics **WHIP** (walks plus hits per inning pitched) and **ERA** (earned run average) are old standbys: WHIP measures walks and hits allowed on a per-inning basis, while ERA measures earned runs on a nine-inning basis. Neither of these stats are translated or adjusted.

DRA- (Deserved Run Average) was described at length earlier, and measures how the pitcher "deserved" to perform compared to other pitchers. Please note that since we lack all the data points that would make for a "real" DRA for minor-league events, the DRA- displayed for minor league partial-seasons is based off of different data. (That data is a modified version of our cFIP metric, which you can find more information about on our website.)

Shane Bieber   RHP

Born: 05/31/95   Age: 26   Bats: R   Throws: R
Height: 6'3"   Weight: 200   Origin: Round 4, 2016 Draft (#122 overall)

YEAR	TEAM	LVL	AGE	W	L	SV	G	GS	IP	H	HR	BB/9	K/9	K	GB%	BABIP
2018	AKR	AA	23	3	0	0	5	5	31	26	1	0.3	8.7	30	47.3%	.278
2018	COL	AAA	23	3	1	0	8	8	48^2	30	3	1.1	8.7	47	52.0%	.227
2018	CLE	MLB	23	11	5	0	20	19	114^2	130	13	1.8	9.3	118	46.2%	.356
2019	CLE	MLB	24	15	8	0	34	33	214^1	186	31	1.7	10.9	259	44.4%	.298
2020	CLE	MLB	25	8	1	0	12	12	77^1	46	7	2.4	14.2	122	48.4%	.267
2021 FS	CLE	MLB	26	10	6	0	26	26	150	121	18	2.1	11.7	195	45.5%	.297
2021 DC	CLE	MLB	26	14	7	0	30	30	196.7	159	24	2.1	11.7	257	45.5%	.297

Comparables: Luis Severino, Danny Salazar, Joe Musgrove

YEAR	TEAM	LVL	AGE	WHIP	ERA	DRA-	WARP	MPH	FB%	WHF	CSP
2018	AKR	AA	23	0.87	1.16	61	0.9				
2018	COL	AAA	23	0.74	1.66	69	1.2				
2018	CLE	MLB	23	1.33	4.55	74	2.6	94.7	57.4%	26.2%	
2019	CLE	MLB	24	1.05	3.28	75	4.9	94.4	45.8%	30.8%	
2020	CLE	MLB	25	0.87	1.63	53	2.6	95.3	53.6%	40.7%	
2021 FS	CLE	MLB	26	1.04	2.44	64	4.4	94.7	50.0%	33.2%	44.2%
2021 DC	CLE	MLB	26	1.04	2.44	64	5.8	94.7	50.0%	33.2%	44.2%

Just like with hitters, **WARP** (Wins Above Replacement Player) is a total value metric that puts pitchers of all stripes on the same scale as position players. We use DRA as the primary input for our calculation of WARP. You might notice that relief pitchers (due to their limited innings) may have a lower WARP than you were expecting or than you might see in other WARP-like metrics. WARP does not take leverage into account, just the actions a pitcher performs and the expected value of those actions ... which ends up judging high-leverage relief pitchers differently than you might imagine given their prestige and market value.

MPH gives you the pitcher's 95th percentile velocity for the noted season, in order to give you an idea of what the *peak* fastball velocity a pitcher possesses. Since this comes from our pitch-tracking data, it is not publicly available for minor-league pitchers.

Finally, we display the three new pitching metrics we described earlier. **FB%** (fastball percentage) gives you the percentage of fastballs thrown out of all pitches. **WHF** (whiff rate) tells you the percentage of swinging strikes induced out of all pitches. **CSP** (called strike probability) expresses the likelihood of all pitches thrown to result in a called strike, after controlling for factors like handedness, umpire, pitch type, count and location.

PECOTA

All players have PECOTA projections for 2021, as well as a set of other numbers that describe the performance of comparable players according to PECOTA. All projections for 2021 are for the player at the date we went to press in early January and are projected into the league and park context as indicated by the team abbreviation. (Note that players at very low levels of the minors are too unpredictable to assess using these numbers.) All PECOTA projected statistics represent a player's projected major-league performance.

How we're doing that is a little different this season. There are really two different values that go into the final stat line that you see for PECOTA: How a player performs, and how much playing time he'll be given to perform it. In the past we've estimated playing time based on each team's roster and depth charts, and we'll continue to do that. These projections are denoted as **2021 DC**.

But in many cases, a player won't be projected for major-league playing time; most of the time this is because they aren't projected to be major-league players at all, but still developing as prospects. Or perhaps a player will provide Triple-A depth, only to have an opportunity open up because of injury. For these purposes, we're also supplying a second projection, labeled **2021 FS**, or full season. This is what we would project the player to provide in 600 plate appearances or 150 innings pitched.

Below the projections are the player's three highest-scoring comparable players as determined by PECOTA. All comparables represent a snapshot of how the listed player was performing at the same age as the current player, so if a

23-year-old pitcher is compared to Bartolo Colón, he's actually being compared to a 23-year-old Colón, not the version that pitched for the Rangers in 2018, nor to Colón's career as a whole.

A few points about pitcher projections. First, we aren't yet projecting peak velocity, so that column will be blank in the PECOTA lines. Second, projecting DRA is trickier than evaluating past performance, because it is unclear how deserving each pitcher will be of his anticipated outcomes. However, we know that another DRA-related statistic–contextual FIP or cFIP-estimates future run scoring very well. So for PECOTA, the projected DRA- figures you see are based on the past cFIPs generated by the pitcher and comparable players over time, along with the other factors described above.

If you're familiar with PECOTA, then you'll have noticed that the projection system often appears bullish on players coming off a bad year and bearish on players coming off a good year. (This is because the system weights several previous seasons, not just the most recent one.) In addition, we publish the 50th percentile projections for each player–which is smack in the middle of the range of projected production—which tends to mean PECOTA stat lines don't often have extreme results like 40 home runs or 250 strikeouts in a given season. In essence, PECOTA doesn't project very many extreme seasons.

Managers

After all those wonderful team chapters, we've got statistics for each big-league manager, all of whom are organized by alphabetical order. Here you'll find a block including an extraordinary amount of information collected from each manager's entire career. For more information on the acronyms and what they mean, please visit the Glossary at www.baseballprospectus.com.

There is one important metric that we'd like to call attention to, and you'll find it next to each manager's name: **wRM+** (weighted reliever management plus). Developed by Rob Arthur and Rian Watt, wRM+ investigates how good a manager is at using their best relievers during the moments of highest leverage, using both our proprietary DRA metric as well as Leverage Index. wRM+ is scaled to a league average of 100, and a wRM+ of 105 indicates that relievers were used approximately five percent "better" than average. On the other hand, a wRM+ of 95 would tell us the team used its relievers five percent "worse" than the average team.

While wRM+ does not have an extremely strong correlation with a manager, it is statistically significant; this means that a manager is not *entirely* responsible for a team's wRM+, but does have some effect on that number.

Part 1: Team Analysis

Performance Graphs

Payroll History (in millions)

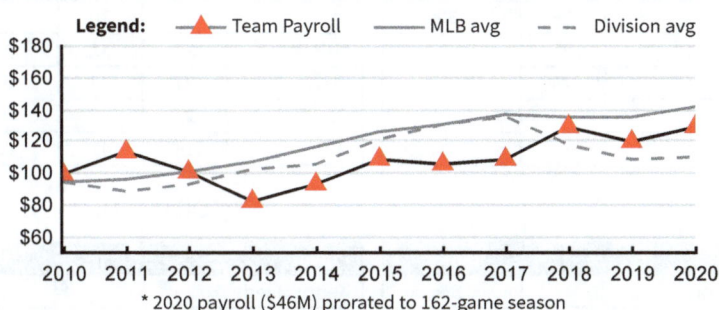

* 2020 payroll ($46M) prorated to 162-game season

Future Commitments (in millions)

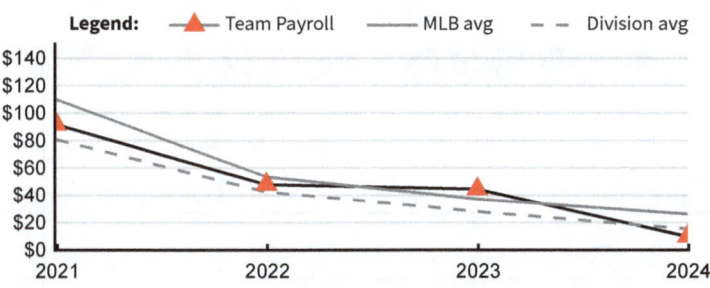

Farm System Ranking

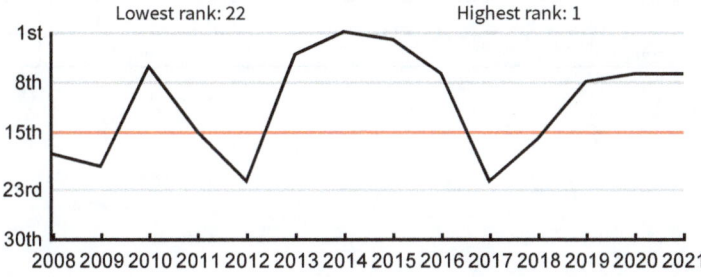

2020 Team Performance

ACTUAL STANDINGS

Team	W	L	Pct
MIN	**36**	**24**	**0.600**
CHW	35	25	0.583
CLE	35	25	0.583
KC	26	34	0.433
DET	23	35	0.397

dWIN% STANDINGS

Team	W	L	Pct
CLE	30	30	0.506
MIN	**29**	**31**	**0.498**
CHW	27	33	0.456
KC	24	36	0.403
DET	19	41	0.333

TOP HITTERS

Player	WARP
Byron Buxton	1.5
Nelson Cruz	1.4
Eddie Rosario	1.4

TOP PITCHERS

Player	WARP
Kenta Maeda	1.5
José Berríos	0.9
Randy Dobnak	0.6

VITAL STATISTICS

Statistic Name	Value	Rank
Pythagenpat	.601	5th
dWin%	.498	10th
Runs Scored per Game	4.48	18th
Runs Allowed per Game	3.58	3rd
Deserved Runs Created Plus	104	9th
Deserved Run Average Minus	94	11th
Fielding Independent Pitching	3.83	3rd
Defensive Efficiency Rating	.706	8th
Batter Age	29.4	21st
Pitcher Age	29.9	21st
Payroll	$46.0M	21st
Marginal $ per Marginal Win	$1.6M	5th

2021 Team Projections

PROJECTED STANDINGS

Team	W	L	Pct	+/-
MIN	**90.8**	**71.2**	**0.560**	**-6**
With Nelson Cruz returning and Andrelton Simmons, J.A. Happ, and Alex Colomé on board the Twins seem like a balanced behemoth again.				
CLE	85.0	77.0	0.525	-9
That they've lost so many great players is an indictment of ownership. That they remain respectable is a testament to the agility of the front office.				
CHW	82.8	79.2	0.511	-11
Lance Lynn and Liam Hendriks give Tony La Russa the paint-by-numbers pitching staff he prefers, and all of the crucial cogs in last year's young lineup return.				
KC	71.5	90.5	0.441	1
Creeping back toward respectability, the Royals added reliable veterans coming off down years and will hope their youth movement gains momentum quickly.				
DET	65.7	96.3	0.406	3
The trend arrow is finally pointing up, but Robbie Grossman and Wilson Ramos qualifying as significant improvements shows they still have a long way to go.				

TOP PROJECTED HITTERS

Player	WARP
Max Kepler	3.2
Josh Donaldson	2.9
Nelson Cruz	2.6

TOP PROJECTED PITCHERS

Player	WARP
Kenta Maeda	4.3
José Berríos	2.8
Michael Pineda	1.8

FARM SYSTEM REPORT

Top Prospect	Number of Top 101 Prospects
Royce Lewis, #31	3

KEY DEDUCTIONS

Player	WARP
Eddie Rosario	2.3
Trevor May	0.8
Matt Wisler	0.5
Sean Poppen	0.3
LaMonte Wade Jr	0.3

KEY ADDITIONS

Player	WARP
J.A. Happ	1.8
Andrelton Simmons	1.5
Hansel Robles	0.4
Alex Colomé	0.4
Shaun Anderson	0.3

Team Personnel

Executive Vice President, Chief Baseball Officer
Derek Falvey

Senior Vice President, General Manager
Thad Levine

Vice President, Assistant General Manager
Rob Antony

Vice President, Player Personnel
Mike Radcliff

Manager
Rocco Baldelli

BP Alumni
Ezra Wise

Target Field Stats

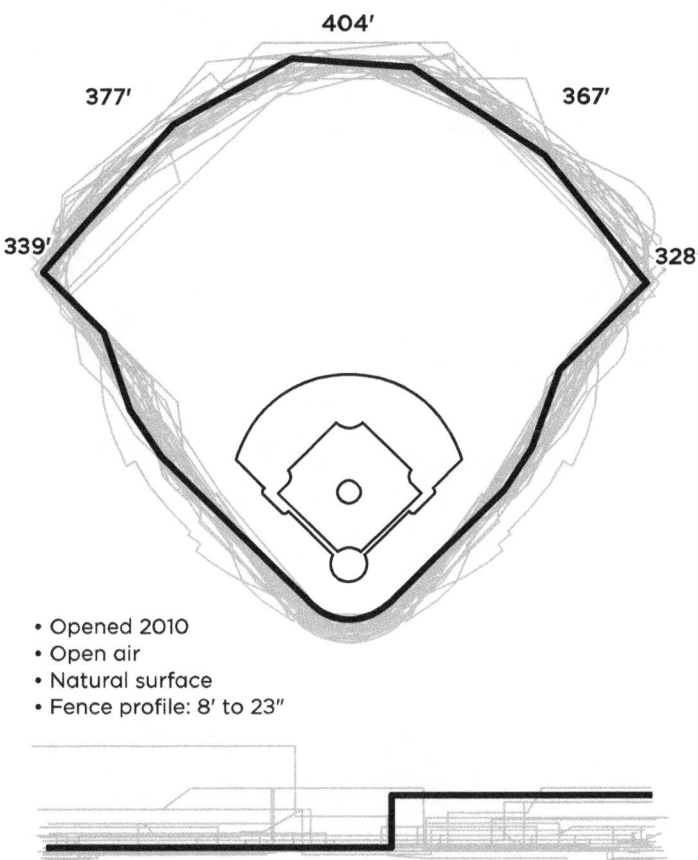

- Opened 2010
- Open air
- Natural surface
- Fence profile: 8' to 23"

Three-Year Park Factors

Runs	Runs/RH	Runs/LH	HR/RH	HR/LH
99	99	101	98	98

Twins Team Analysis

Curses are part of the mystique of baseball. The 2004 season saw the end of one of the most infamous of those alleged maledictions: The Curse of the Bambino. Its victims, the Boston Red Sox, exorcised their demons the night of October 27, when they swept the St. Louis Cardinals to win their first World Series title in 86 years.

One could argue that the curse ended a week earlier, in Game 7 of the American League Championship Series, when Boston completed a historic comeback from a 3-0 deficit in the best-of-seven series, something no other team in professional sports has accomplished before or since. That the comeback happened in the Bronx, against the Yankees, the team at the opposite end of the Bambino's curse, was poetic.

Those who dabble in the occult, and even those who don't, might fancy the idea that a new curse saw its genesis in the Bronx during that same postseason.

A few weeks before the Red Sox completed their historic comeback, a left-hander with a wipeout changeup by the name of Johan Santana took the mound for the Minnesota Twins for Game 1 of the American League Division Series. Santana, who would claim his first AL Cy Young Award the following month, shut out the Yankees while striking out five to help the Twins kick off the playoffs with a 2-0 win.

Unless you've been living under a rock (and given the way 2020 unfolded, no one would blame you for it), you are likely aware that something extraordinary has happened in the 16 years since Santana's gem: The Twins have played 18 postseason games in that span, including three more against the Yankees in that 2004 ALDS, and somehow, inexplicably and maddeningly, they have managed to lose every single one of them.

With their loss in Game 1 of the 2020 American League Wild Card Series against the Astros, the Twins' postseason losing streak stretched to 17 games, which made it not just the longest active streak across all North American professional sports, but the longest in the *history* of North American pro sports. The Twins extended their run of misery to 18 losses a day later, and were summarily swept out of the playoffs.

Here's what that list looks like at the moment:

- **Minnesota Twins:** 18 games (2004- present)
- **Chicago Blackhawks:** 16 games (1975-79)

- **Detroit Pistons:** 14 games (2008- present)
- **Los Angeles Kings:** 14 games (1993-2001)
- **Boston Red Sox:** 13 games (1986-1995)
- **New York Knicks:** 13 games (2001-2012)

To put the streak in perspective, when it began Twins legend Joe Mauer was still a rookie. Rocco Baldelli, the club's current manager, was 22 years old and coming off his second full season in the majors. Second baseman Luis Arráez was seven years old. And perhaps most mind-blowing: Ageless wonder Nelson Cruz, the nap-loving 40-year-old slugger who paced the 2020 Twins with 16 home runs and a .992 OPS, *had not yet made his Major League debut.*

The historic dimensions of Minnesota's playoffs woes are stunning enough that we should go ahead and say it: The Twins are cursed.

You might point to the Curse of the Bambino and argue that 16 years is a drop in the bucket when it comes to baseball droughts. The Chicago Cubs, who went 108 years between their most recent titles as a result of a curse that's been pinned on a goat, would agree. And Cleveland has not won a Fall Classic since 1948, the longest active drought in the majors, and we don't go around saying they are cursed. (Though maybe we should?)

Still, it's much easier to wrap one's mind around extended playoff and championship droughts than around 18 consecutive postseason losses. Winning a World Series requires an alchemical blend of talent, depth, health and luck. Winning a single game? That is a simpler endeavor. Sometimes, a hit that falls unexpectedly or an errant throw will suffice. Even while mired in their respective curses, the Red Sox and Cubs won postseason games and series. The math supports that observation: Using FiveThirty Eight's Elo ratings, folks at the Harvard Sports Analysis Collective calculated that Minnesota's odds of losing 18 consecutive games were 0.002 percent, or about 1 in 54,000.

Of the Twins 18 straight postseason losses, 13 (!) have come at the hands of the Yankees. Then there's the fact that the Twins held the lead at some point in 11 of those 18 losses while also being outscored 107-48 during the streak. Consider also that 28 of the other 29 Major League Baseball teams (the Seattle Mariners are the other exception) have won at least one postseason game since Santana stifled the Yankees on October 5, 2004.

Some of those 18 losses have been more frustrating than others. If you are looking for evidence of a curse, your best fodder might be Game 2 of the 2009 ALDS against—who else—the Yankees. In that contest, what might have been a leadoff double by Mauer down the left field line in the top of the 11th inning, with the score tied at 3-3, was instead ruled a foul ball by umpire Phil Cuzzi. Mauer wound up on base with a single, and Minnesota followed with a couple more singles after that, but they ultimately did not score, and the Yankees walked off in the bottom of the frame.

It's worth nothing that much has changed for the Twins in the last 16 years, and not just as far the roster is concerned. In 2010, they abandoned the aging Hubert H. Humphrey Metrodome for Target Field. And once perceived as lagging behind in the analytics revolution that has redefined many aspects of the game, in recent years they have become one of the most forward-thinking in that regard, from the front office to the dugout. Yet none of those changes has translated into even a solitary postseason win.

The Twins' historic postseason misery is a sobering reminder that, even with all the number crunching in the world, baseball—and October baseball in particular—remains defiant in its ability to humble you. Said Cruz after the Twins were eliminated by the Astros, "Like life, baseball is also tough. It's unpredictable."

⚾ ⚾ ⚾

Curses are meant to be broken, and entering 2020, the Twins appeared poised to do just that. After pacing the American League with 307 in home runs in 2019, a season that was defined by record-setting power across the majors, and winning a franchise-record 101 games, the self-proclaimed "Bomba Squad" added more thump by signing slugging third baseman Josh Donaldson to the largest contract in franchise history. Pitching also became a strength for the Twins thanks largely to the acquisition of Kenta Maeda, who went 6-1 with a 2.70 ERA in 11 starts in 2020 and finished second in the voting for the AL Cy Young Award.

And for once, a playoff matchup seemed to favor Minnesota, which came into the AL Wild Card Series as the favorites over the maligned Astros, who, less than a year removed from their sign-stealing scandal, made the postseason despite posting a losing record. Houston did so without its ace, Justin Verlander, and after having lost Gerrit Cole to free agency over the winter.

But in the end, Bomba Squad 2.0 could not capitalize on the circumstances. Injuries were partly to blame: Because of a calf issue that limited him to 28 regular season games, Donaldson didn't even make the roster for the Wild Card Series. Center fielder Byron Buxton, who was hit in the helmet by a pitch during the last week of the regular season, did not start Game 2.

So, after fending off Cleveland and White Sox to claim their second consecutive American League Central title during a shortened 60-game season due to the COVID-19 pandemic, Minnesota's hitters posted a .119 average and .399 OPS in the AL Wild Card Series on their way to being swept by Houston. In the process, they forfeited what might have been their best shot at making a deep October run with its current core.

But curses aren't broken by the merely obvious or great. They're broken by the resilient. By the people and teams who dare to ask "why not?" We need only look back to 2019, when the Nationals, unable to get out of the NLDS in every instance prior, managed to unseat the powerhouse Dodgers on their way to the first title in franchise history. Was it the best Nationals squad in recent memory? No. Did that stop them? You know the answer.

If the Twins make it back to the playoffs this year, full seasons from a healthy Donaldson and Buxton could be a big reason why. The Twins have their ace in Maeda, who still has three years left on his contract. José Berrios will also be back, with another chance to blossom into the ace-caliber he has long appeared on the brink of becoming.

The 2021 Minnesota Twins will be brimming with young talent, too. Some of those fresh faces arrived in 2020, notably outfielder Alex Kirilloff, who made his big-league debut in Game 2 of the AL Wild Card Series, and became the first position player in Major League Baseball history to record his first career hit in the postseason. Catching prospect Ryan Jeffers, who had a solid debut last year, should be a factor for Minnesota in 2021, as could top pitching prospects Jhoan Duran and Jordan Balazovic. All these young players haven't been around long enough to learn not to ask "why not?"

Of course, to break an 18-game postseason game losing streak, you have to get to the postseason first. And Minnesota's path to October now looks more complicated with the rise of the White Sox as legitimate contenders in the AL Central. The task may have gotten harder, but nothing about breaking curses is supposed to be easy.

—Nathalie Alonso is an editorial producer & reporter @LasMayores, the Spanish-language website for @MLB.

Part 2: Player Analysis

Minnesota Twins 2021

PLAYER COMMENTS WITH GRAPHS

Luis Arraez 2B
Born: 04/09/97   Age: 24   Bats: L   Throws: R
Height: 5'10"   Weight: 175   Origin: International Free Agent, 2013

YEAR	TEAM	LVL	AGE	PA	R	2B	3B	HR	RBI	BB	K	SB	CS	AVG/OBP/SLG
2018	FTM	HI-A	21	258	27	14	3	1	20	19	28	2	3	.320/.373/.421
2018	CHA	AA	21	195	25	6	0	2	16	13	16	2	0	.298/.345/.365
2019	PNS	AA	22	164	18	6	1	0	14	18	13	3	3	.342/.415/.397
2019	ROC	AAA	22	73	8	4	0	0	8	6	2	1	0	.348/.397/.409
2019	MIN	MLB	22	366	54	20	1	4	28	36	29	2	2	.334/.399/.439
2020	MIN	MLB	23	121	16	9	0	0	13	8	11	0	0	.321/.364/.402
2021 FS	MIN	MLB	24	600	69	31	2	8	63	46	70	1	1	.301/.360/.410
2021 DC	MIN	MLB	24	467	54	24	1	6	49	36	55	0	1	.301/.360/.410

Comparables: Dustin Pedroia, Ron Hunt, Gil McDougald

Last season, Arraez became the first player since 2008 to record 100 plate appearances and slug over .400 without hitting a homer (Joaquin Arias was the last to do it). The key to his success is that he's the best contact hitter in the world. Over the past two seasons, nobody has missed less often when they've swung (he has a three percent whiff rate), and he's far and away the best in the game at making contact with balls off the plate (89 percent; next closest is Nick Markakis at 82 percent). It all works because Arraez is more of a spray hitter than a slap hitter, adept at hitting to all fields with just enough doubles power to make outfielders think twice before they creep in. As the only 80-bat, 20-power player in baseball, Arraez is a throwback and a refreshing reminder of the sport's capacity for variance. For however homogeneous this game has gotten in recent years, there will always be a few unicorns in baseball.

YEAR	TEAM	LVL	AGE	PA	DRC+	BABIP	BRR	FRAA	WARP
2018	FTM	HI-A	21	258	130	.356	-2.4	2B(40): 1.7, 3B(6): 0.3, SS(5): 0.3	1.0
2018	CHA	AA	21	195	110	.315	0.0	2B(27): -1.0, 3B(10): 0.3, SS(9): 1.4	0.5
2019	PNS	AA	22	164	176	.376	-0.9	2B(15): -0.1, 3B(15): 4.2, SS(5): 0.5	2.2
2019	ROC	AAA	22	73	129	.354	-0.9	SS(8): 0.4, 2B(4): 1.5, 3B(3): -0.1	0.6
2019	MIN	MLB	22	366	121	.355	2.9	2B(49): -2.8, LF(21): 1.5, 3B(17): -0.2	2.3
2020	MIN	MLB	23	121	114	.353	0.3	2B(31): 1.2	0.7
2021 FS	MIN	MLB	24	600	112	.337	-0.8	2B 0, 3B 1	2.8
2021 DC	MIN	MLB	24	467	112	.337	-0.6	2B 0, 3B 1	2.0

Luis Arraez, continued

Batted Ball Distribution

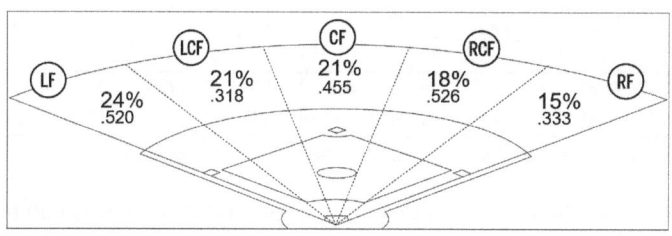

Strike Zone vs LHP   Strike Zone vs RHP

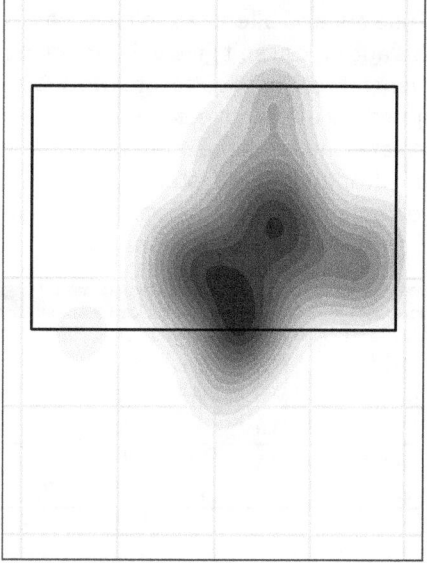

Minnesota Twins 2021

Byron Buxton CF

Born: 12/18/93   Age: 27   Bats: R   Throws: R
Height: 6'2"   Weight: 190   Origin: Round 1, 2012 Draft (#2 overall)

YEAR	TEAM	LVL	AGE	PA	R	2B	3B	HR	RBI	BB	K	SB	CS	AVG/OBP/SLG
2018	ROC	AAA	24	148	22	11	1	4	14	9	42	4	1	.272/.331/.456
2018	MIN	MLB	24	94	8	4	0	0	4	3	28	5	0	.156/.183/.200
2019	MIN	MLB	25	295	48	30	4	10	46	19	68	14	3	.262/.314/.513
2020	MIN	MLB	26	135	19	3	0	13	27	2	36	2	1	.254/.267/.577
2021 FS	MIN	MLB	27	600	75	25	4	23	77	39	179	17	5	.231/.288/.424
2021 DC	MIN	MLB	27	474	59	20	3	18	61	31	141	13	4	.231/.288/.424

Comparables: Reggie Taylor, Ryan Thompson, Corey Patterson

Each year, MLB's Playing Rules Committee evaluates how they can make the game a better viewing experience. This year, perhaps they can start by asking themselves "How do we get more Byron Buxtons on the field?"

Buxton is not an efficient ballplayer. The Pete Reiser of his day, Buxton's incredible motor and belligerence toward the outfield wall will simply not allow him to stay in the lineup with any regularity. Between that, his propensity to strike out and allergy to the free pass, he's an incredibly flawed player. And yet, this author doesn't give a damn about any of that. As the three-true-outcome events threaten to suffocate the sport, Buxton's game offers an appealing alternative. More than anyone in this era, Buxton and his elite athleticism break the mold of what we imagine a star to look and play like. With jaw-dropping speed, sterling defense in center and a newfound power stroke, he's a human highlight reel and an avatar for what the game desperately needs more of—and, ideally, more from.

YEAR	TEAM	LVL	AGE	PA	DRC+	BABIP	BRR	FRAA	WARP
2018	ROC	AAA	24	148	103	.367	1.4	CF(28): 9.0	1.3
2018	MIN	MLB	24	94	57	.226	0.3	CF(27): 1.4	0.0
2019	MIN	MLB	25	295	98	.314	4.4	CF(86): 14.2	2.9
2020	MIN	MLB	26	135	114	.241	0.5	CF(39): 8.6	1.5
2021 FS	MIN	MLB	27	600	95	.295	1.7	CF 12	3.0
2021 DC	MIN	MLB	27	474	95	.295	1.4	CF 10	2.4

Byron Buxton, continued

Batted Ball Distribution

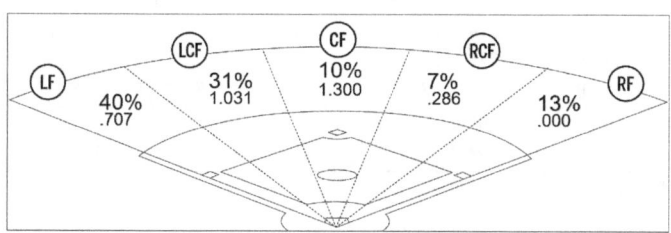

Strike Zone vs LHP   **Strike Zone vs RHP**

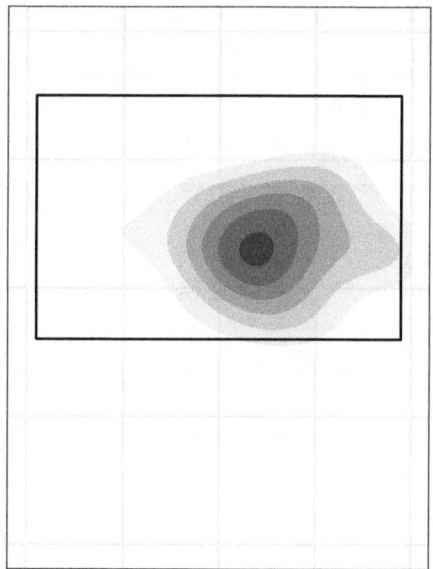

Jake Cave CF

Born: 12/04/92   Age: 28   Bats: L   Throws: L
Height: 6'0"   Weight: 200   Origin: Round 6, 2011 Draft (#209 overall)

YEAR	TEAM	LVL	AGE	PA	R	2B	3B	HR	RBI	BB	K	SB	CS	AVG/OBP/SLG
2018	ROC	AAA	25	250	26	9	1	6	28	26	55	4	2	.269/.352/.403
2018	MIN	MLB	25	309	54	16	2	13	45	18	102	2	1	.265/.313/.473
2019	ROC	AAA	26	214	37	18	4	7	39	15	50	5	0	.352/.393/.592
2019	MIN	MLB	26	228	28	11	2	8	25	21	71	0	0	.258/.351/.455
2020	MIN	MLB	27	123	17	3	2	4	15	5	44	0	2	.221/.285/.389
2021 FS	MIN	MLB	28	600	68	23	4	19	70	42	203	1	1	.226/.293/.392
2021 DC	MIN	MLB	28	194	22	7	1	6	22	13	65	0	0	.226/.293/.392

Comparables: Preston Wilson, Ruben Rivera, Tyler Naquin

Much like this author's work in the kitchen, the holes in Cave's game got exposed in more regular action last year. He slumped early, started pressing, got a little swing happy and ultimately pitchers were able to coax more chases on balls out of the strike zone than in years past. Lefties in particular ate his lunch, striking him out 15 times in 32 at-bats. It would be premature to use these struggles as evidence to suggest that one of baseball's best fourth outfielders can't hack it in everyday duty; we're only talking about 40 games, and 2020 is not the best year to draw big conclusions from. For now though, the Twins will be happy to return him to his usual post as a weapon off the bench and an insurance policy for Byron Buxton's inevitable bouts with the center field wall.

YEAR	TEAM	LVL	AGE	PA	DRC+	BABIP	BRR	FRAA	WARP
2018	ROC	AAA	25	250	114	.327	-0.1	RF(36): 5.4, CF(17): -0.6, LF(6): 1.6	1.3
2018	MIN	MLB	25	309	93	.363	3.1	CF(70): -7.5, RF(11): 0.3, LF(4): -0.5	0.3
2019	ROC	AAA	26	214	140	.437	1.1	CF(37): -3.5, RF(7): -0.8	1.3
2019	MIN	MLB	26	228	89	.358	1.3	RF(45): -1.7, CF(23): 0.2, LF(10): 0.4	0.3
2020	MIN	MLB	27	123	69	.323	-0.3	CF(22): -3.1, RF(12): 0.6, LF(7): 0.0	-0.4
2021 FS	MIN	MLB	28	600	87	.320	-0.2	CF -3, LF 2	0.6
2021 DC	MIN	MLB	28	194	87	.320	-0.1	CF -1, LF 1	0.2

Jake Cave, continued

Batted Ball Distribution

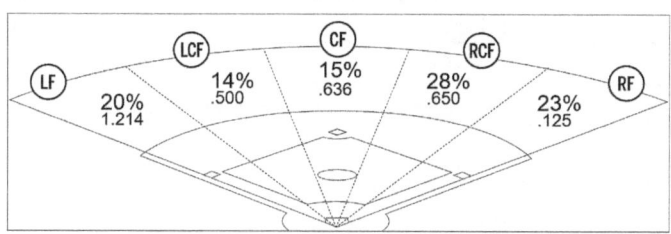

Strike Zone vs LHP   Strike Zone vs RHP

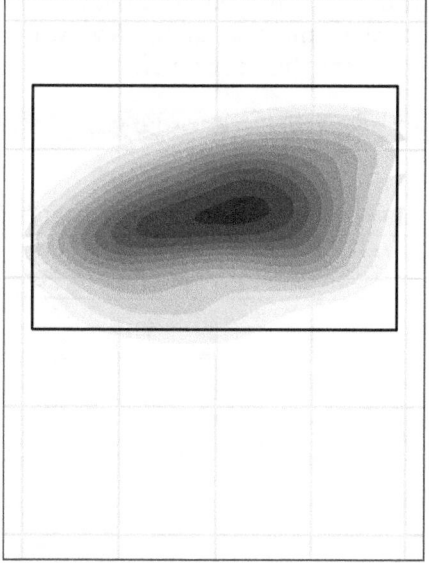

Twins Player Analysis - 19

Nelson Cruz DH

Born: 07/01/80 Age: 41 Bats: R Throws: R
Height: 6'2" Weight: 230 Origin: International Free Agent, 1998

YEAR	TEAM	LVL	AGE	PA	R	2B	3B	HR	RBI	BB	K	SB	CS	AVG/OBP/SLG
2018	SEA	MLB	37	591	70	18	1	37	97	55	122	1	0	.256/.342/.509
2019	MIN	MLB	38	521	81	26	0	41	108	56	131	0	1	.311/.392/.639
2020	MIN	MLB	39	214	33	6	0	16	33	25	58	0	0	.303/.397/.595
2021 FS	MIN	MLB	40	600	88	22	0	31	96	59	174	1	1	.249/.334/.479
2021 DC	MIN	MLB	40	553	81	21	0	29	88	54	160	1	1	.249/.334/.479

Comparables: Reggie Jackson, Matt Stairs, Reggie Sanders

Cruz may not be the greatest old player in recent memory—Barry Bonds springs to mind—but at a time when 33 passes for old, he is the game's premier elder statesman. Turning 40 didn't slow him down a bit, as he slugged above .500 for the eighth year running and was on pace for yet another 40-homer season. Despite the monster year, you can squint and see the faintest signs of decline. His average exit velocity dropped, and using Statcast metrics, both his batting average and slugging percentage were higher than expected based on the quality of his contact. Still, even if Cruz is finally on the back half of the mountain, there are quite a few switchbacks between him and sea level. He should earn his keep for another year or two.

YEAR	TEAM	LVL	AGE	PA	DRC+	BABIP	BRR	FRAA	WARP
2018	SEA	MLB	37	591	131	.264	-1.2	RF(4): 0.1	3.1
2019	MIN	MLB	38	521	151	.351	-1.0		4.1
2020	MIN	MLB	39	214	141	.360	-0.7		1.4
2021 FS	MIN	MLB	40	600	125	.304	-0.9	RF 0	3.1
2021 DC	MIN	MLB	40	553	125	.304	-0.9		2.6

Nelson Cruz, continued

Batted Ball Distribution

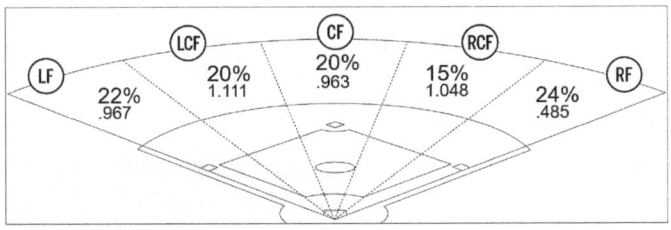

Strike Zone vs LHP   Strike Zone vs RHP

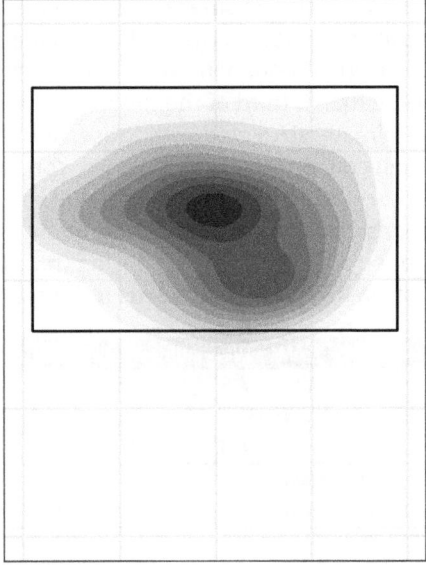

Twins Player Analysis - 21

Mitch Garver C

Born: 01/15/91 Age: 30 Bats: R Throws: R
Height: 6'1" Weight: 220 Origin: Round 9, 2013 Draft (#260 overall)

YEAR	TEAM	LVL	AGE	PA	R	2B	3B	HR	RBI	BB	K	SB	CS	AVG/OBP/SLG
2018	MIN	MLB	27	335	38	19	2	7	45	29	72	0	0	.268/.335/.414
2019	MIN	MLB	28	359	70	16	1	31	67	41	87	0	0	.273/.365/.630
2020	MIN	MLB	29	81	8	1	0	2	5	7	37	0	0	.167/.247/.264
2021 FS	MIN	MLB	30	600	82	25	1	26	76	62	192	0	1	.231/.316/.436
2021 DC	MIN	MLB	30	312	43	13	0	13	39	32	100	0	0	.231/.316/.436

Comparables: Jorge Posada, Todd Hundley, Rick Wilkins

YEAR	TEAM	P. COUNT	FRM RUNS	BLK RUNS	THRW RUNS	TOT RUNS
2018	MIN	11863	-8.2	0.2	-0.4	-8.4
2019	MIN	11037	4.2	-0.3	-0.4	3.5
2020	MIN	2772	-0.6	-0.1	0.0	-0.8
2021	MIN	10822	-4.6	-0.3	0.0	-4.9
2021	MIN	10822	-4.6	-0.2	0.0	-4.9

Garver must have gotten drunk on power in 2019 because last year he looked like he had a bad hangover. There are many reasons his production fell so dramatically, but one that stands out is his performance on fastballs. In 2019, he hit over .300, slugged .800 and smacked 25 dingers against the heater. His whiff rate against the pitch was a bit high, but not notably so. In 2020 though, he went from missing 15 percent of fastballs to whiffing more than a third of the time. He also missed offspeed pitches more often, but he already struggled with those, and it's the performance against heaters that is most concerning going forward. You can survive in the big leagues while flailing at curveballs, but you won't if you can't catch up to the cheese. Whether last year's crash stemmed from an intercostal strain, a launch angle that might have tipped a bit too high for a swing that starts so flat or just the worst run of 80 at-bats in his life, Garver needs to forget this nightmare ever happened.

YEAR	TEAM	LVL	AGE	PA	DRC+	BABIP	BRR	FRAA	WARP
2018	MIN	MLB	27	335	99	.330	-1.3	C(86): -8.5, 1B(5): -0.1, P(1): -0.0	0.5
2019	MIN	MLB	28	359	148	.277	-0.7	C(82): 4.7, 1B(1): -0.0	4.4
2020	MIN	MLB	29	81	56	.294	-0.3	C(22): 0.6, 1B(1): -0.0	-0.3
2021 FS	MIN	MLB	30	600	110	.304	-0.8	C -6, 1B 0	2.5
2021 DC	MIN	MLB	30	312	110	.304	-0.4	C -5	1.2

Mitch Garver, continued

Batted Ball Distribution

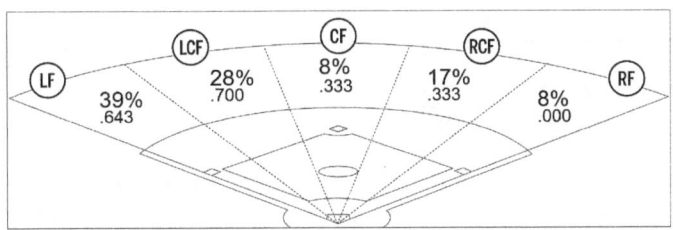

Strike Zone vs LHP   **Strike Zone vs RHP**

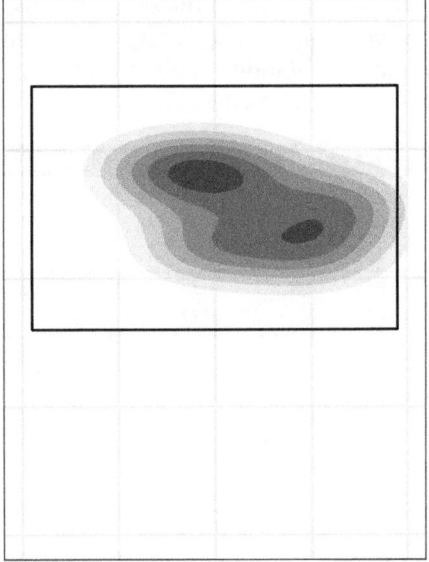

Marwin Gonzalez 3B

Born: 03/14/89 Age: 32 Bats: S Throws: R
Height: 6'1" Weight: 205 Origin: International Free Agent, 2005

YEAR	TEAM	LVL	AGE	PA	R	2B	3B	HR	RBI	BB	K	SB	CS	AVG/OBP/SLG
2018	HOU	MLB	29	552	61	25	3	16	68	53	126	2	3	.247/.324/.409
2019	MIN	MLB	30	463	52	19	0	15	55	31	98	1	0	.264/.322/.414
2020	MIN	MLB	31	199	15	4	0	5	22	17	41	0	0	.211/.286/.320
2021 FS	MIN	MLB	32	600	64	28	1	18	69	46	139	6	4	.250/.317/.406
2021 DC	MIN	MLB	32	424	45	20	0	12	49	32	98	4	3	.250/.317/.406

Comparables: Jhonny Peralta, Ian Desmond, Asdrúbal Cabrera

Not only did Gonzalez apologize and express remorse for his part in Houston's Banging Scheme, but he actually seemed to mean it (which gave him a leg up on some of his former teammates and two legs up on the rest). It's hard to let him off the hook entirely though, because it seems increasingly likely that he benefited substantially from the con. After a down 2019, Gonzalez cratered in 2020. He's a .248/.311/.387 hitter since leaving the Astros, and the discipline he displayed while laying off wayward breaking balls and changeups back in 2017-18 evaporated the second he bid adieu to Harris County's most lopsided garbage can. He's still rosterable given his positional flexibility, but any remaining plaudits of his late-blooming batting acumen should probably be thrown in the trash.

YEAR	TEAM	LVL	AGE	PA	DRC+	BABIP	BRR	FRAA	WARP
2018	HOU	MLB	29	552	100	.301	1.5	LF(73): 0.7, SS(39): -2.7, 2B(32): -0.2	1.6
2019	MIN	MLB	30	463	91	.310	-1.2	RF(44): -4.8, 3B(40): 5.0, 1B(21): 0.7	1.1
2020	MIN	MLB	31	199	90	.241	-1.2	3B(23): -1.0, 2B(21): -1.1, 1B(14): -0.3	-0.3
2021 FS	MIN	MLB	32	600	99	.305	-0.3	2B -2, 3B 1	1.1
2021 DC	MIN	MLB	32	424	99	.305	-0.2	2B -1, 3B 0	0.9

Marwin Gonzalez, continued

Batted Ball Distribution

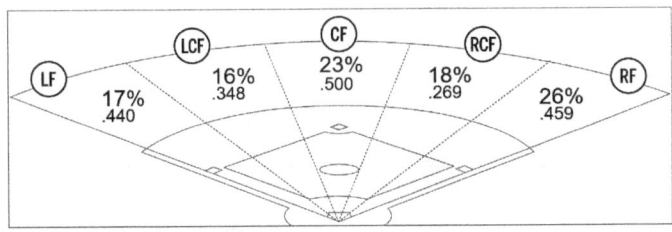

Strike Zone vs LHP **Strike Zone vs RHP**

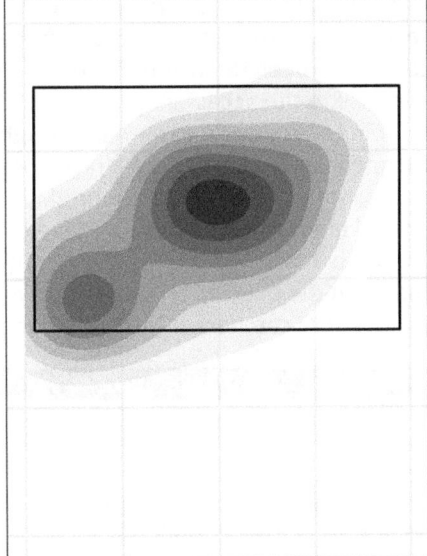

Ryan Jeffers C

Born: 06/03/97 Age: 24 Bats: R Throws: R
Height: 6'4" Weight: 235 Origin: Round 2, 2018 Draft (#59 overall)

YEAR	TEAM	LVL	AGE	PA	R	2B	3B	HR	RBI	BB	K	SB	CS	AVG/OBP/SLG
2018	ELZ	ROK	21	129	29	7	0	3	16	20	16	0	1	.422/.543/.578
2018	CR	LO-A	21	155	19	10	0	4	17	14	30	0	0	.288/.361/.446
2019	FTM	HI-A	22	315	35	11	0	10	40	28	64	0	0	.256/.330/.402
2019	PNS	AA	22	99	13	5	0	4	9	9	19	0	0	.287/.374/.483
2020	MIN	MLB	23	62	5	0	0	3	7	5	19	0	0	.273/.355/.436
2021 FS	MIN	MLB	24	600	77	25	1	19	72	49	168	0	1	.244/.317/.408
2021 DC	MIN	MLB	24	276	35	11	0	9	33	22	77	0	0	.244/.317/.408

Comparables: Devin Mesoraco, Danny Jansen, Jake Fox

It took just two seasons for Jeffers to vault from the second round of the draft to starting catcher on a playoff team. Part of that was a function of timing: Mitch Garver and Alex Aliva forgot how to hit and a virus of modest renown hamstrung Minnesota's efforts

YEAR	TEAM	P. COUNT	FRM RUNS	BLK RUNS	THRW RUNS	TOT RUNS
2019	PNS	2243	-0.3	0.0	-0.4	-0.7
2020	MIN	2804	0.3	-0.1	0.1	0.3
2021	MIN	10822	0.6	-0.6	-0.8	-0.7
2021	MIN	10822	0.6	-1.3	-0.8	-1.4

to find a proven replacement. The Twins rolled the dice on Jeffers and did he ever rise to the occasion. It was only 23 games but he hit well down the stretch, bringing his power into games enough to offset the swing-and-miss issues that prospect analysts accurately prognosticated. Perhaps more importantly, he demonstrated that his receiving skills have grown considerably since college, and all but put to bed any lingering concerns that he'll have to move to first base soon. He doesn't have the world's highest ceiling and he'll need to prove he can maintain the power as the league acclimates to him, but it's starting to look like Minnesota's catcher of the future has arrived ahead of schedule.

YEAR	TEAM	LVL	AGE	PA	DRC+	BABIP	BRR	FRAA	WARP
2018	ELZ	ROK	21	129		.482			
2018	CR	LO-A	21	155	144	.343	0.4	C(22): 0.2	1.2
2019	FTM	HI-A	22	315	121	.297	-2.7	C(57): 0.7	1.6
2019	PNS	AA	22	99	142	.328	1.4	C(17): -0.9	0.8
2020	MIN	MLB	23	62	92	.364	-0.5	C(25): -0.1	0.1
2021 FS	MIN	MLB	24	600	102	.317	-0.9	C -1	2.5
2021 DC	MIN	MLB	24	276	102	.317	-0.4	C 0	1.1

Ryan Jeffers, continued

Batted Ball Distribution

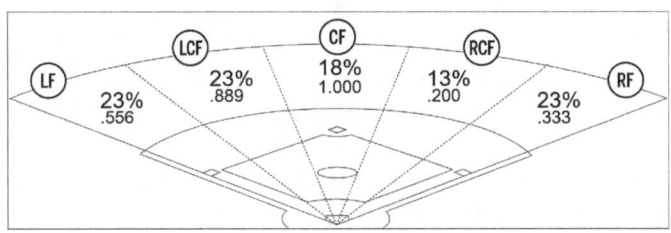

Strike Zone vs LHP **Strike Zone vs RHP**

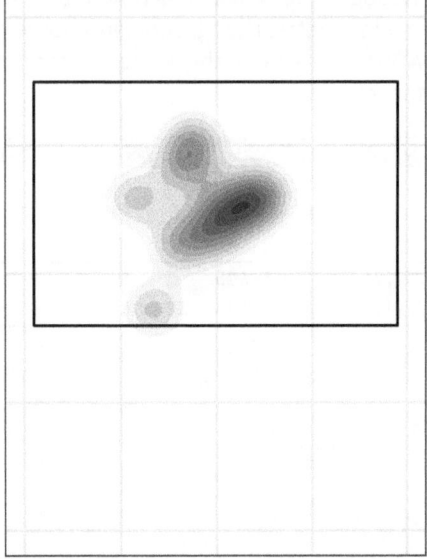

Max Kepler RF

Born: 02/10/93 Age: 28 Bats: L Throws: L
Height: 6'4" Weight: 225 Origin: International Free Agent, 2009

YEAR	TEAM	LVL	AGE	PA	R	2B	3B	HR	RBI	BB	K	SB	CS	AVG/OBP/SLG
2018	MIN	MLB	25	611	80	30	4	20	58	71	96	4	5	.224/.319/.408
2019	MIN	MLB	26	596	98	32	0	36	90	60	99	1	5	.252/.336/.519
2020	MIN	MLB	27	196	27	9	0	9	23	22	36	3	0	.228/.321/.439
2021 FS	MIN	MLB	28	600	89	28	2	26	69	67	119	5	3	.245/.337/.458
2021 DC	MIN	MLB	28	620	92	29	2	26	71	69	123	5	3	.245/.337/.458

Comparables: Jeremy Hermida, Michael Cuddyer, Brennan Boesch

If you're looking for a player who embodies the "first-division regular" descriptor, Kepler fits the bill perfectly. Arguably the league's most graceful player, he posted another productive campaign at the plate with his trademark good defense in right field. The one knock on his game? BABIP, of all things. Among players with 2,000 PA's over the last five years, only Todd Frazier and Albert Pujols are under Kepler's .252 mark. Given his relatively high launch angle and pedestrian exit velocity, a low BABIP isn't totally surprising. Nevertheless, as a speedy lefty who has reached base less often than his batted-tracking metrics suggest he should've throughout his career, he's due for a BABIP spike one of these years. When it comes, he'll deserve a spot on the All-Star team.

YEAR	TEAM	LVL	AGE	PA	DRC+	BABIP	BRR	FRAA	WARP
2018	MIN	MLB	25	611	102	.236	2.7	RF(117): 10.2, CF(55): -1.3	2.9
2019	MIN	MLB	26	596	125	.244	-3.7	RF(84): 6.0, CF(60): -3.6	3.5
2020	MIN	MLB	27	196	114	.236	-0.3	RF(44): -2.7, CF(2): -0.4	0.3
2021 FS	MIN	MLB	28	600	119	.270	-0.2	RF 4, CF 0	3.3
2021 DC	MIN	MLB	28	620	119	.270	-0.3	RF 4, CF 0	3.2

Max Kepler, continued

Batted Ball Distribution

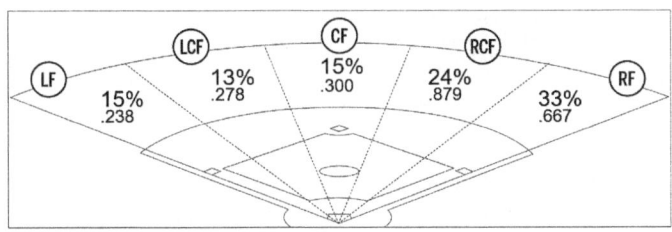

Strike Zone vs LHP **Strike Zone vs RHP**

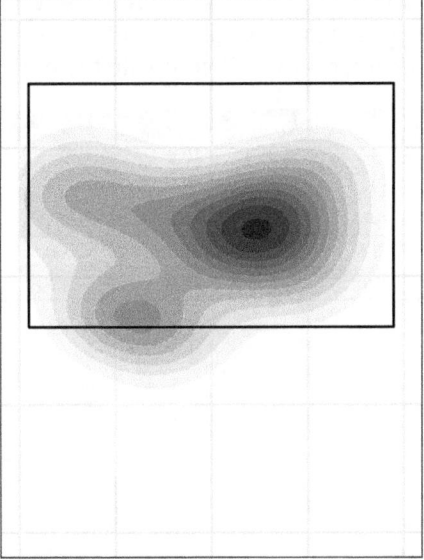

Jorge Polanco SS

Born: 07/05/93   Age: 28   Bats: S   Throws: R
Height: 5'11"   Weight: 208   Origin: International Free Agent, 2009

YEAR	TEAM	LVL	AGE	PA	R	2B	3B	HR	RBI	BB	K	SB	CS	AVG/OBP/SLG
2018	MIN	MLB	24	333	38	18	3	6	42	25	62	7	7	.288/.345/.427
2019	MIN	MLB	25	704	107	40	7	22	79	60	116	4	3	.295/.356/.485
2020	MIN	MLB	26	226	22	8	0	4	19	13	35	4	2	.258/.304/.354
2021 FS	MIN	MLB	27	600	75	29	4	15	71	46	106	8	4	.261/.322/.414
2021 DC	MIN	MLB	27	603	75	29	4	15	71	46	107	8	4	.261/.322/.414

Comparables: Angel Berroa, Jeff Blauser, Khalil Greene

Polanco moving off shortstop has always seemed a matter of when, not if, given his sub-par glove at the six. A career-worst slash line appears disastrous in that context, except DRC+ was far more generous and Polanco turned in an almost error-free performance to convince the majority of the defensive metrics that he was average—if not better—with the glove. Whether we can believe that over a sample of barely 50 games is another matter. Talk about him moving to a super-utility role suggests the team is inclined to disregard it. Minnesota would prefer that he go back to the five-win level of performance that made his current contract look like a stroke of genius. As long as he's an average regular in some regard, they won't complain too much about how he gets there.

YEAR	TEAM	LVL	AGE	PA	DRC+	BABIP	BRR	FRAA	WARP
2018	MIN	MLB	24	333	97	.345	-3.0	SS(76): -9.7	0.1
2019	MIN	MLB	25	704	119	.328	4.9	SS(142): -0.7	5.3
2020	MIN	MLB	26	226	102	.292	-0.6	SS(53): 1.7	0.8
2021 FS	MIN	MLB	27	600	102	.299	0.4	SS 0	2.0
2021 DC	MIN	MLB	27	603	102	.299	0.4	2B 0, SS 0	2.0

Jorge Polanco, continued

Batted Ball Distribution

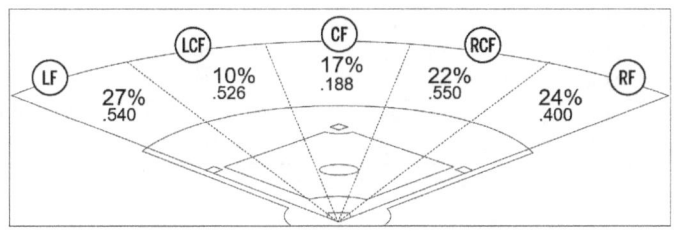

Strike Zone vs LHP

Strike Zone vs RHP

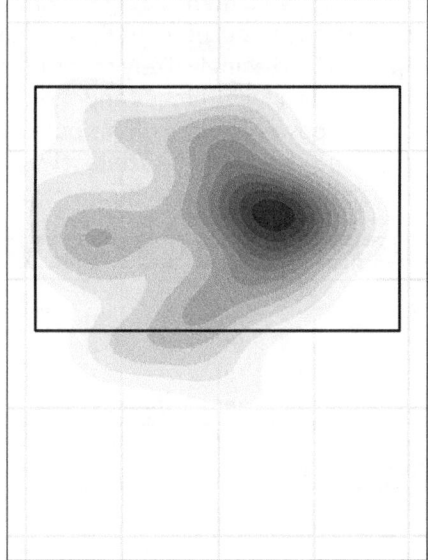

Minnesota Twins 2021

Miguel Sanó 3B
Born: 05/11/93   Age: 28   Bats: R   Throws: R
Height: 6'4"   Weight: 272   Origin: International Free Agent, 2009

YEAR	TEAM	LVL	AGE	PA	R	2B	3B	HR	RBI	BB	K	SB	CS	AVG/OBP/SLG
2018	FTM	HI-A	25	77	11	2	0	2	12	13	21	0	0	.328/.442/.453
2018	ROC	AAA	25	36	2	1	0	2	5	6	8	0	0	.267/.389/.500
2018	MIN	MLB	25	299	32	14	0	13	41	31	115	0	0	.199/.281/.398
2019	MIN	MLB	26	439	76	19	2	34	79	55	159	0	1	.247/.346/.576
2020	MIN	MLB	27	205	31	12	0	13	25	18	90	0	0	.204/.278/.478
2021 FS	MIN	MLB	28	600	85	24	1	33	90	71	246	0	1	.224/.318/.472
2021 DC	MIN	MLB	28	502	71	20	1	28	75	59	206	0	1	.224/.318/.472

Comparables: Mark Reynolds, Russell Branyan, Chris Carter

Sanó continued his Hosmerian pattern of following a promising season with a clunker, headlined by a strikeout rate that would embarrass Mark Reynolds. Is it too early to call Sanó's career a dissapointment? It sounds premature, and to be fair, the "bust" label would clearly be a step too far: He's made an All-Star team, compiled eight career WARP and deserves his place in the middle of a pretty good lineup. Still, there's a significant gap between the 70-grade star scouts projected and the useful but flawed player he's become. With each passing year, it appears increasingly likely that this is the real Sanó: A good, not great, hitter who will mash for stretches and then slump horribly for weeks at a time. He has too much power to write off his potential entirely, but as a bad-bodied 27-year-old with no speed and less defensive value, there's a chance Sanó's best baseball is already behind him.

YEAR	TEAM	LVL	AGE	PA	DRC+	BABIP	BRR	FRAA	WARP
2018	FTM	HI-A	25	77	162	.463	0.2	3B(10): 0.4	0.6
2018	ROC	AAA	25	36	129	.300	0.2	3B(4): 1.5, 1B(1): -0.0	0.3
2018	MIN	MLB	25	299	82	.286	-1.0	3B(56): 0.1, 1B(11): 0.1	0.2
2019	MIN	MLB	26	439	127	.319	-2.5	3B(91): -3.2, 1B(9): -0.6	2.5
2020	MIN	MLB	27	205	91	.301	1.7	1B(52): -3.5	-0.2
2021 FS	MIN	MLB	28	600	118	.336	-0.8	1B -1, 3B 0	2.2
2021 DC	MIN	MLB	28	502	118	.336	-0.7	1B -1	1.7

Miguel Sanó, continued

Batted Ball Distribution

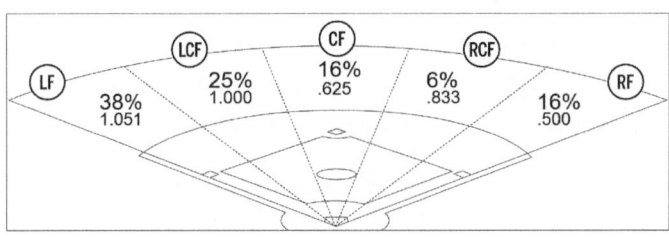

Strike Zone vs LHP   Strike Zone vs RHP

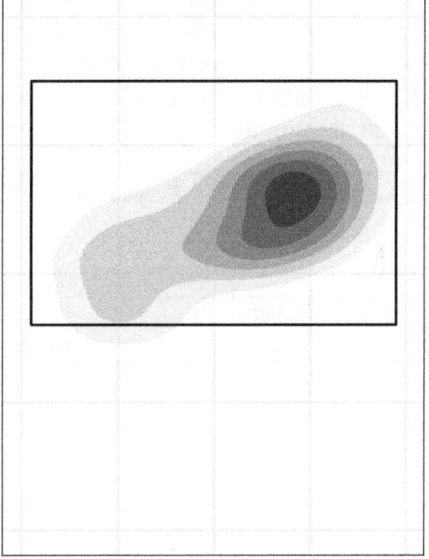

Andrelton Simmons SS
Born: 09/04/89 Age: 31 Bats: R Throws: R
Height: 6'2" Weight: 195 Origin: Round 2, 2010 Draft (#70 overall)

YEAR	TEAM	LVL	AGE	PA	R	2B	3B	HR	RBI	BB	K	SB	CS	AVG/OBP/SLG
2018	LAA	MLB	28	600	68	26	5	11	75	35	44	10	2	.292/.337/.417
2019	LAA	MLB	29	424	47	19	0	7	40	24	37	10	2	.264/.309/.364
2020	LAA	MLB	30	127	19	7	0	0	10	8	16	2	0	.297/.346/.356
2021 FS	MIN	MLB	31	600	69	30	2	9	64	40	72	11	5	.272/.326/.387
2021 DC	MIN	MLB	31	528	60	26	1	8	56	35	63	10	4	.272/.326/.387

Comparables: Orlando Cabrera, Julio Franco, Ramon Martinez

The phrase "thirtysomething shortstop" is almost an oxymoron at this point. In 2020, two of the top 19 shortstops in baseball, according to WARP, were 30 years of age or older. In 2019, none cracked the top 20. Simmons' defense has been and remains his calling card, despite increasing noise about his efficacy where once the metrics sang in harmonious acclaim. In his first taste of free agency after a blueprint-making team-friendly contract, it's Simmons' offensive abilities that will give prospective suitors pause. After a few seasons in which it appeared he'd turned a corner from his slap-hitting youth, "Simba" has regressed at the plate, if not quite to the bug-eating extremity of his movie counterpart. Still excellent at making contact, Simmons will have to stop showing that talent off, especially on pitches out of the zone, if he wants to match his animated equivalent's triumphant third act.

YEAR	TEAM	LVL	AGE	PA	DRC+	BABIP	BRR	FRAA	WARP
2018	LAA	MLB	28	600	106	.300	3.8	SS(145): -6.8	2.9
2019	LAA	MLB	29	424	80	.277	-0.1	SS(102): 10.5	2.0
2020	LAA	MLB	30	127	84	.343	0.6	SS(30): 1.4	0.3
2021 FS	MIN	MLB	31	600	97	.298	0.3	SS 1	1.8
2021 DC	MIN	MLB	31	528	97	.298	0.3	SS 1	1.5

Andrelton Simmons, continued

Batted Ball Distribution

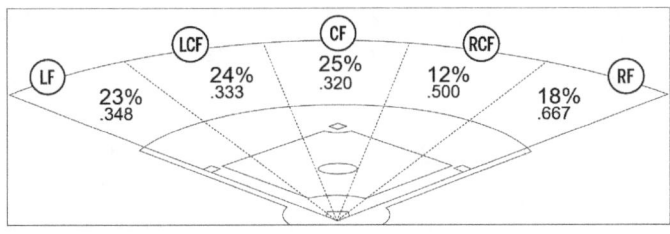

Strike Zone vs LHP   Strike Zone vs RHP

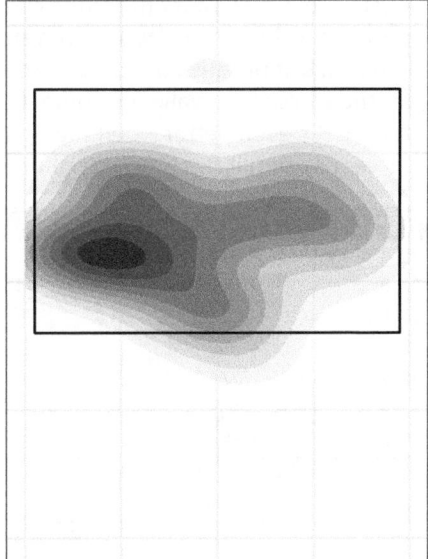

Jorge Alcala   RHP

Born: 07/28/95   Age: 25   Bats: R   Throws: R
Height: 6'3"   Weight: 205   Origin: International Free Agent, 2014

YEAR	TEAM	LVL	AGE	W	L	SV	G	GS	IP	H	HR	BB/9	K/9	K	GB%	BABIP
2018	FAY	HI-A	22	1	4	2	10	7	38^2	25	2	4.2	10.5	45	45.7%	.256
2018	CC	AA	22	2	3	1	9	5	40^2	36	1	3.8	8.2	37	40.9%	.310
2018	CHA	AA	22	0	4	0	5	4	20	23	4	6.3	9.9	22	31.7%	.339
2019	PNS	AA	23	5	7	0	26	16	102^2	114	12	3.2	9.2	105	37.6%	.355
2019	ROC	AAA	23	1	0	0	5	0	7^2	4	0	2.3	12.9	11	53.3%	.267
2019	MIN	MLB	23	0	0	0	2	0	1^2	1	0	5.4	5.4	1	0.0%	.200
2020	MIN	MLB	24	2	1	0	16	0	24	21	3	3.0	10.1	27	39.0%	.321
2021 FS	MIN	MLB	25	2	2	0	57	0	50	45	6	4.7	9.6	53	38.4%	.295
2021 DC	MIN	MLB	25	2	2	0	55	0	56.7	52	7	4.7	9.6	60	38.4%	.295

Comparables: Hector Perez, Robert Dugger, Hunter Wood

The planet, country and sport of baseball are all barely recognizable vestiges of what we all took for granted five years ago. In this strange and less hospitable environment, it's nice to depend on certain things, no matter how trifling. This brings us to Alcala. At a time when even obscure prospects are seemingly six months of weighted-ball work from stardom, it's good that we can still count on some wild but promising righties to get a modest velocity bump in the bullpen after the whole five-walks-per-nine thing got them kicked out of a Triple-A rotation. It's even better when that in turn leads to a big-league promotion and a career of solid (if rarely spectacular) relief work.

YEAR	TEAM	LVL	AGE	WHIP	ERA	DRA-	WARP	MPH	FB%	WHF	CSP
2018	FAY	HI-A	22	1.11	3.03	70	0.9				
2018	CC	AA	22	1.30	3.54	83	0.5				
2018	CHA	AA	22	1.85	5.85	107	0.0				
2019	PNS	AA	23	1.47	5.87	129	-1.8				
2019	ROC	AAA	23	0.78	0.00	38	0.3				
2019	MIN	MLB	23	1.20	0.00	118	0.0	97.1	65.5%	35.7%	
2020	MIN	MLB	24	1.21	2.62	87	0.4	99.4	46.4%	32.2%	
2021 FS	MIN	MLB	25	1.44	4.54	102	0.2	99.3	47.3%	32.4%	46.2%
2021 DC	MIN	MLB	25	1.44	4.54	102	0.2	99.3	47.3%	32.4%	46.2%

Jorge Alcala, continued

Pitch Shape vs LHH

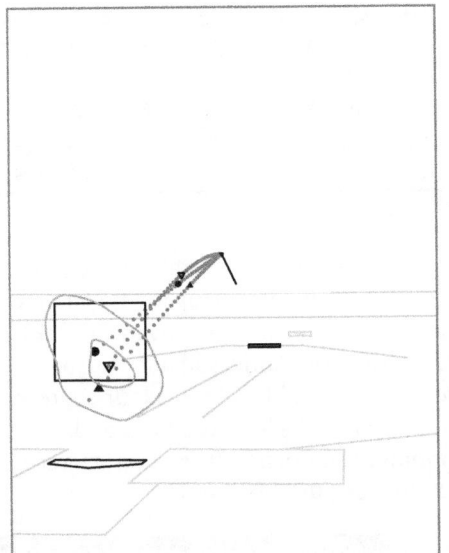

Pitch Shape vs RHH

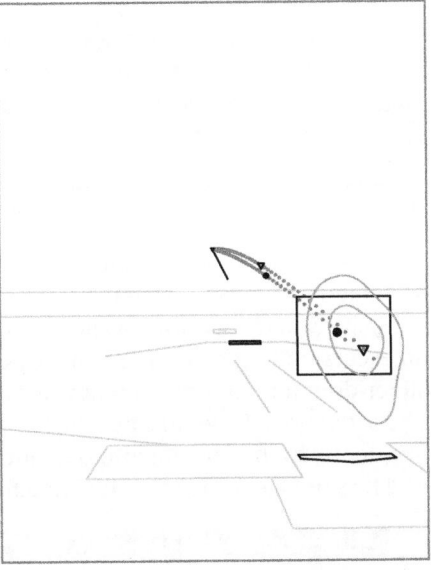

Type	Frequency	Velocity	H Movement	V Movement
● Fastball	46.2%	97.1 [114]	-6.6 [101]	-10.8 [112]
▲ Changeup	8.9%	89.3 [116]	-15.2 [82]	-22.4 [114]
▽ Slider	44.7%	88.7 [121]	3.3 [93]	-27.4 [119]

Shaun Anderson   RHP

Born: 10/29/94   Age: 26   Bats: R   Throws: R
Height: 6'4"   Weight: 228   Origin: Round 3, 2016 Draft (#88 overall)

YEAR	TEAM	LVL	AGE	W	L	SV	G	GS	IP	H	HR	BB/9	K/9	K	GB%	BABIP
2018	RIC	AA	23	6	5	0	17	16	94	93	9	2.1	8.9	93	46.9%	.318
2018	SAC	AAA	23	2	2	0	8	8	47^1	48	5	2.1	6.5	34	43.2%	.295
2019	SAC	AAA	24	2	1	0	8	8	38^1	36	3	3.1	9.6	41	53.3%	.320
2019	SF	MLB	24	3	5	2	28	16	96	111	13	3.6	6.6	70	39.7%	.327
2020	SF	MLB	25	0	0	0	18	0	15^1	10	3	7.0	10.6	18	37.8%	.206
2021 FS	MIN	MLB	26	9	8	0	26	26	150	145	22	3.5	8.4	139	43.0%	.291
2021 DC	MIN	MLB	26	4	4	0	38	6	46.7	45	7	3.5	8.4	43	43.0%	.291

Comparables: Walker Lockett, Drew Anderson, Justin Grimm

Sometimes the obvious story is the accurate one. Absent a viable third pitch, Anderson was moved from the rotation to the 'pen in late 2019, and he pitched exclusively in relief during a shortened season which was made even shorter by an excursion to the Alternate Site. Out of the bullpen, Anderson adopted a slider-dominant approach that was offset with a credible mid-90s four-seamer. The slider gets the whiffs, but the heater gets bashed a little too hard and frequently for him to slot into the ninth inning. The upshot: he's not a starter and he's not a closer; he's a just-fine bullpen piece until he's not.

YEAR	TEAM	LVL	AGE	WHIP	ERA	DRA-	WARP	MPH	FB%	WHF	CSP
2018	RIC	AA	23	1.22	3.45	60	2.7				
2018	SAC	AAA	23	1.25	4.18	89	0.7				
2019	SAC	AAA	24	1.28	3.76	60	1.4				
2019	SF	MLB	24	1.55	5.44	133	-0.8	95.1	58.5%	20.8%	
2020	SF	MLB	25	1.43	3.52	108	0.1	96.6	39.7%	33.6%	
2021 FS	MIN	MLB	26	1.36	4.38	102	1.3	95.4	54.6%	23.5%	45.2%
2021 DC	MIN	MLB	26	1.36	4.38	102	0.3	95.4	54.6%	23.5%	45.2%

Shaun Anderson, continued

Pitch Shape vs LHH	Pitch Shape vs RHH
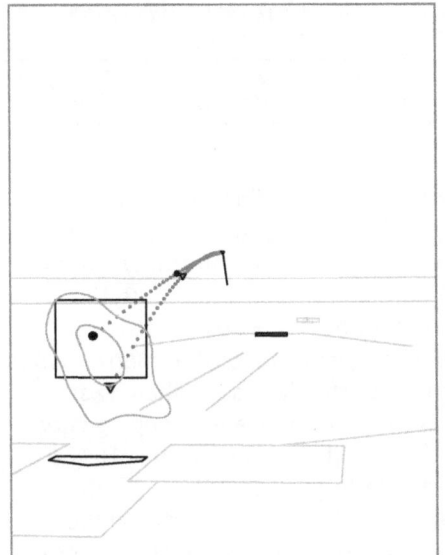	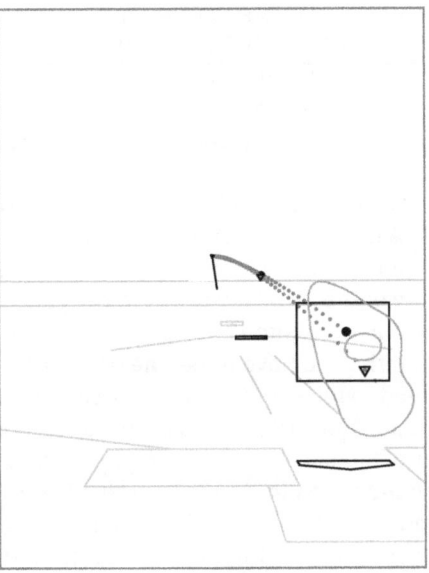

Type	Frequency	Velocity	H Movement	V Movement
● Fastball	39.4%	94.5 [106]	-1.7 [124]	-13.6 [105]
▲ Changeup	6.8%	87.7 [110]	-9.1 [114]	-26.7 [102]
▽ Slider	53.0%	88.3 [119]	5.2 [100]	-28.8 [114]

José Berríos RHP

Born: 05/27/94   Age: 27   Bats: R   Throws: R
Height: 6'0"   Weight: 205   Origin: Round 1, 2012 Draft (#32 overall)

YEAR	TEAM	LVL	AGE	W	L	SV	G	GS	IP	H	HR	BB/9	K/9	K	GB%	BABIP
2018	MIN	MLB	24	12	11	0	32	32	192^1	159	25	2.9	9.5	202	40.7%	.271
2019	MIN	MLB	25	14	8	0	32	32	200^1	194	26	2.3	8.8	195	41.9%	.301
2020	MIN	MLB	26	5	4	0	12	12	63	57	8	3.7	9.7	68	40.2%	.295
2021 FS	MIN	MLB	27	10	7	0	26	26	150	135	19	3.1	9.4	157	41.3%	.291
2021 DC	MIN	MLB	27	11	9	0	29	29	174.7	157	23	3.1	9.4	183	41.3%	.291

Comparables: Jake Odorizzi, Zach Davies, Luke Weaver

Is Berríos an ace? The answer depends on how you define the term. While DRA isn't quite as enamored with his production as other third-order metrics, four consecutive durable years of sub-100 DRA- baseball comfortably makes him one of the 30 best starters in the game. On the scouting side of things, the definition tightens up considerably. To earn the "ace" label by the strictest criteria, you have to be one of the 10ish best pitchers and for that, Berríos would need to take another step forward. Catch him on the right day, when he's dotting his fastball and flummoxing hitters with the comically sweeping curve, and it looks possible. In the long run, we think he'll settle below that. He's a wee-bit too hittable to be a true No. 1, particularly given that the ungodly movement on his pitches leads to a fair amount of walks and traffic on the bases. None of this should be interpreted as a knock: No. 2 starters don't grow on trees and Berríos is fun as hell to watch. The Twins have a great one here, and fans should hope Derek Falvey and company are able to keep him in town for years to come.

YEAR	TEAM	LVL	AGE	WHIP	ERA	DRA-	WARP	MPH	FB%	WHF	CSP
2018	MIN	MLB	24	1.14	3.84	94	2.4	95.2	60.4%	26.0%	
2019	MIN	MLB	25	1.22	3.68	91	2.9	94.8	55.2%	23.3%	
2020	MIN	MLB	26	1.32	4.00	90	0.9	96.2	51.5%	27.4%	
2021 FS	MIN	MLB	27	1.24	3.71	88	2.4	95.3	55.5%	25.0%	47.8%
2021 DC	MIN	MLB	27	1.24	3.71	88	2.8	95.3	55.5%	25.0%	47.8%

José Berríos, continued

Pitch Shape vs LHH

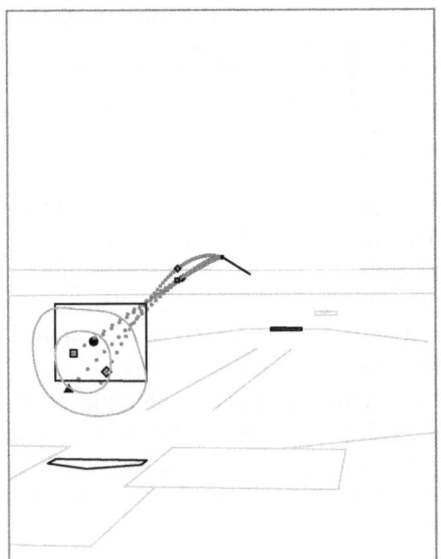

Pitch Shape vs RHH

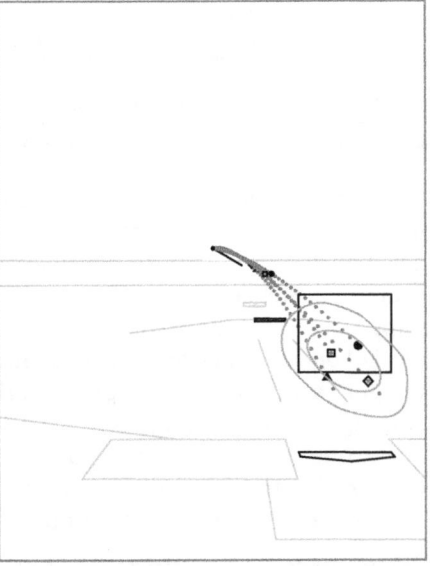

Type	Frequency	Velocity	H Movement	V Movement
● Fastball	25.2%	94.7 [107]	-9.4 [87]	-13.8 [104]
☐ Sinker	26.2%	94.2 [109]	-14 [93]	-18.3 [107]
▲ Changeup	18.8%	84.9 [99]	-11 [104]	-30.3 [92]
◇ Curveball	29.8%	83.5 [119]	13.2 [123]	-37.6 [124]

Tyler Clippard   RHP

Born: 02/14/85 Age: 36 Bats: R Throws: R
Height: 6'3" Weight: 200 Origin: Round 9, 2003 Draft (#274 overall)

YEAR	TEAM	LVL	AGE	W	L	SV	G	GS	IP	H	HR	BB/9	K/9	K	GB%	BABIP
2018	TOR	MLB	33	4	3	7	73	1	68²	57	13	3.0	11.1	85	20.0%	.275
2019	CLE	MLB	34	1	0	0	53	3	62	38	8	2.2	9.3	64	31.0%	.207
2020	MIN	MLB	35	2	1	0	26	2	26	19	2	1.4	9.0	26	29.4%	.258
2021 FS	MIN	MLB	36	2	2	0	57	0	50	41	7	3.2	9.4	52	29.2%	.262
2021 DC	MIN	MLB	36	2	2	0	54	0	46.7	38	7	3.2	9.4	48	29.2%	.262

Comparables: Pedro Strop, Michael Gonzalez, Brian Fuentes

There were 35 pitchers who suited up for the 2011 All-Star Game. One of them is no longer with us. Two are in the Hall of Fame. Twenty-five were out of baseball in 2020. Only four are anywhere near as good now as they were nine years ago: Michael Pineda, Clayton Kershaw, Justin Verlander and Tyler Clippard. Intuitively, we all understand that it's hard to maintain such a high level of performance for a decade, but in the context of his All-Star peers, Clippard's run looks downright remarkable. There aren't many signs that he's slowing down, either. He just notched his third consecutive season with a WHIP below one and 11th straight year with an above average DRA-. He's maybe not the sexiest pitcher around (glasses notwithstanding) but history will remember him as one of the more under-appreciated players of the 2010s.

YEAR	TEAM	LVL	AGE	WHIP	ERA	DRA-	WARP	MPH	FB%	WHF	CSP
2018	TOR	MLB	33	1.17	3.67	79	1.1	92.5	42.6%	31.7%	
2019	CLE	MLB	34	0.85	2.90	84	0.8	91.2	40.8%	28.2%	
2020	MIN	MLB	35	0.88	2.77	97	0.3	90.5	38.0%	28.3%	
2021 FS	MIN	MLB	36	1.18	3.46	85	0.6	91.4	40.5%	29.2%	46.2%
2021 DC	MIN	MLB	36	1.18	3.46	85	0.6	91.4	40.5%	29.2%	46.2%

Tyler Clippard, continued

Pitch Shape vs LHH	Pitch Shape vs RHH
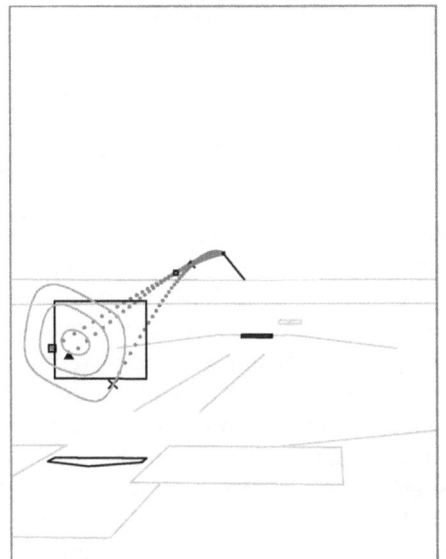	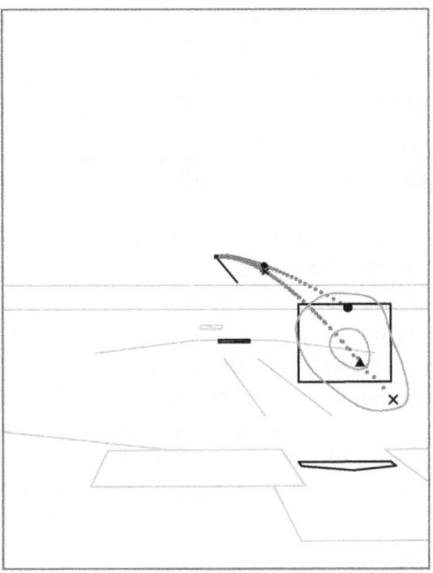

Type	Frequency	Velocity	H Movement	V Movement
● Fastball	19.2%	89.6 [91]	-6.1 [103]	-13 [106]
□ Sinker	18.8%	88.9 [82]	-11 [115]	-16.6 [113]
▲ Changeup	34.6%	78.1 [73]	-12.1 [98]	-26.8 [102]
✕ Splitter	19.2%	81.3 [82]	0.4 [131]	-39.6 [66]
◇ Curveball	7.0%	75.2 [87]	5.5 [91]	-53.1 [90]

Alex Colomé RHP
Born: 12/31/88   Age: 32   Bats: R   Throws: R
Height: 6'1"   Weight: 225   Origin: International Free Agent, 2007

YEAR	TEAM	LVL	AGE	W	L	SV	G	GS	IP	H	HR	BB/9	K/9	K	GB%	BABIP
2018	TB	MLB	29	2	5	11	23	0	21²	24	1	3.3	9.6	23	54.5%	.354
2018	SEA	MLB	29	5	0	1	47	0	46¹	35	6	2.5	9.5	49	42.5%	.254
2019	CHW	MLB	30	4	5	30	62	0	61	42	7	3.4	8.1	55	44.1%	.217
2020	CHW	MLB	31	2	0	12	21	0	22¹	13	0	3.2	6.4	16	51.6%	.203
2021 FS	MIN	MLB	32	2	2	20	57	0	50	46	6	3.4	8.4	46	45.7%	.287
2021 DC	MIN	MLB	32	3	3	20	65	0	56.7	53	7	3.4	8.4	53	45.7%	.287

Comparables: Adam Warren, Sean Marshall, Sam LeCure

The man who took a PED suspension for a horse steroid and flipped it into making "The Horse" his Players Weekend nickname naturally applied his flair for absurd literalism to his job the past two years. The White Sox traded for Colomé with the expectation that he would get outs and convert saves. He has converted 42 out of 46 saves since 2019, and he's gotten about 74 percent of opposing hitters out. They did not acquire him to get outs in a traditionally sustainable way, so he eschewed that element of his performance. They did not acquire him to come in and blow everyone away, and lend a bunch of confidence to the idea that he can do that every time, or that every save he records isn't reliant on a light sprinkling of defensive heroics, so he didn't do it. Maybe, in private pre-series meetings, they told him to flip in his 89-90 mph cutter over and over again that every hitter tries to swat to the moon but rolls over to third base instead, because that is like, *all* he does.

YEAR	TEAM	LVL	AGE	WHIP	ERA	DRA-	WARP	MPH	FB%	WHF	CSP
2018	TB	MLB	29	1.48	4.15	87	0.3	95.9	36.8%	30.4%	
2018	SEA	MLB	29	1.04	2.53	88	0.5	96.7	49.3%	30.0%	
2019	CHW	MLB	30	1.07	2.80	81	0.9	95.8	29.0%	29.1%	
2020	CHW	MLB	31	0.94	0.81	91	0.3	95.9	28.4%	30.9%	
2021 FS	MIN	MLB	32	1.31	4.05	96	0.4	96.1	33.0%	29.9%	44.7%
2021 DC	MIN	MLB	32	1.31	4.05	96	0.4	96.1	33.0%	29.9%	44.7%

Alex Colomé, continued

Pitch Shape vs LHH	Pitch Shape vs RHH
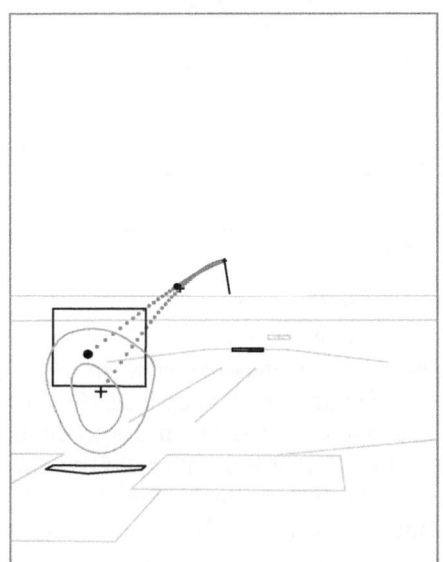	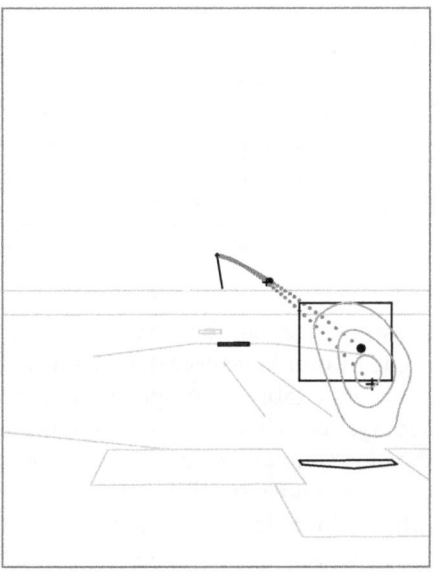

Type	Frequency	Velocity	H Movement	V Movement
● Fastball	28.4%	94.6 [106]	-2.2 [122]	-12 [109]
+ Cutter	71.6%	89.5 [108]	3.6 [111]	-25.2 [96]

Minnesota Twins 2021

Randy Dobnak RHP
Born: 01/17/95 Age: 26 Bats: R Throws: R
Height: 6'1" Weight: 230 Origin: Undrafted Free Agent, 2017

YEAR	TEAM	LVL	AGE	W	L	SV	G	GS	IP	H	HR	BB/9	K/9	K	GB%	BABIP
2018	CR	LO-A	23	10	5	0	24	20	129	138	6	1.7	5.9	84	46.0%	.318
2019	FTM	HI-A	24	3	0	0	4	4	22^1	18	0	1.6	5.6	14	57.6%	.273
2019	PNS	AA	24	4	2	0	11	10	66^2	58	6	0.8	8.2	61	59.1%	.281
2019	ROC	AAA	24	5	2	0	9	7	46	28	0	3.5	6.7	34	60.2%	.220
2019	MIN	MLB	24	2	1	1	9	5	28^1	27	1	1.6	7.3	23	54.0%	.302
2020	MIN	MLB	25	6	4	0	10	10	46^2	50	3	2.5	5.2	27	61.0%	.311
2021 FS	MIN	MLB	26	9	8	0	26	26	150	156	16	3.3	6.6	109	57.1%	.300
2021 DC	MIN	MLB	26	4	4	0	35	11	52	54	5	3.3	6.6	38	57.1%	.300

Comparables: Kevin Gausman, Aaron Sanchez, Jhoulys Chacín

Dobnak's time in the spotlight came in 2019, and given that he went from substitute teacher to Marty Bystrom in the course of six months, it's hard to argue he didn't deserve it. While he actually pitched somewhat worse in 2020—inevitably, really, given the surface-level stats he racked up in 2019—10 average starts in his second spin through the league carries a lot more credibility than four miraculous ones out of nowhere. The low strikeout rate gives us some concern, but we're still pretty confident that he'll slot into the back-end of a rotation for at least a few seasons. He's what passes for a pitch-to-contact hurler these days, and while it seems a little off-key for a guy with Dobnak's background to wind up as a generic no. 4 starter, it sure beats the hell out of teaching algebra.

YEAR	TEAM	LVL	AGE	WHIP	ERA	DRA-	WARP	MPH	FB%	WHF	CSP
2018	CR	LO-A	23	1.26	3.14	109	0.1				
2019	FTM	HI-A	24	0.99	0.40	77	0.3				
2019	PNS	AA	24	0.96	2.56	75	1.0				
2019	ROC	AAA	24	1.00	2.15	50	1.8				
2019	MIN	MLB	24	1.13	1.59	94	0.3	94.5	59.0%	27.0%	
2020	MIN	MLB	25	1.35	4.05	91	0.6	93.5	48.5%	20.6%	
2021 FS	MIN	MLB	26	1.41	4.40	101	1.3	93.7	51.4%	22.4%	46.1%
2021 DC	MIN	MLB	26	1.41	4.40	101	0.4	93.7	51.4%	22.4%	46.1%

Randy Dobnak, continued

Pitch Shape vs LHH	Pitch Shape vs RHH
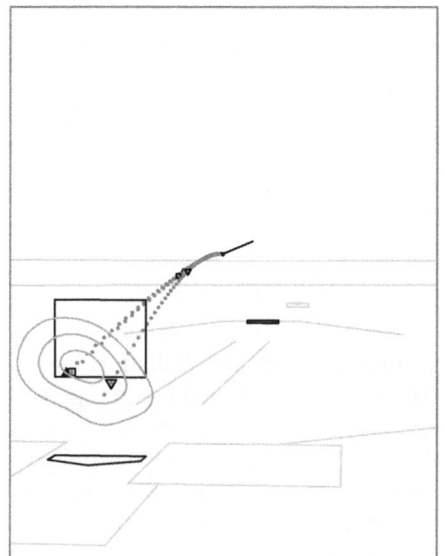	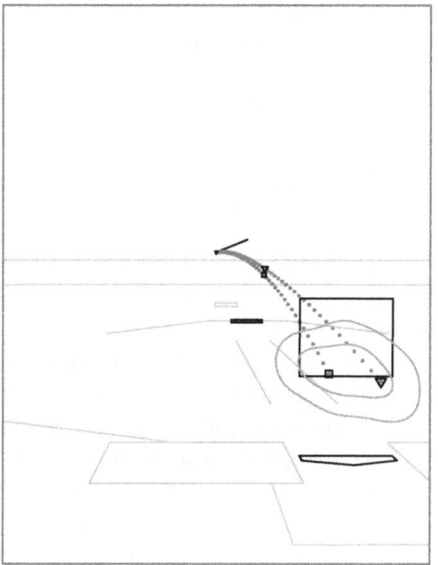

Type	Frequency	Velocity	H Movement	V Movement
● Fastball	4.4%	93.2 [102]	-9.7 [86]	-21.2 [83]
☐ Sinker	44.1%	91.6 [96]	-13.3 [98]	-29.9 [70]
▲ Changeup	16.2%	85.8 [102]	-13.9 [88]	-30.5 [92]
▽ Slider	35.3%	83.6 [99]	1.4 [85]	-34.9 [97]

Tyler Duffey RHP

Born: 12/27/90   Age: 30   Bats: R   Throws: R
Height: 6'3"   Weight: 220   Origin: Round 5, 2012 Draft (#160 overall)

YEAR	TEAM	LVL	AGE	W	L	SV	G	GS	IP	H	HR	BB/9	K/9	K	GB%	BABIP
2018	ROC	AAA	27	4	4	3	31	0	59	48	5	3.1	9.6	63	42.5%	.283
2018	MIN	MLB	27	2	2	0	19	1	25	26	6	1.4	6.8	19	34.9%	.260
2019	ROC	AAA	28	0	0	1	7	0	13²	8	0	3.3	14.5	22	44.0%	.333
2019	MIN	MLB	28	5	1	0	58	0	57²	44	8	2.2	12.6	81	36.2%	.275
2020	MIN	MLB	29	1	1	0	22	0	24	13	2	2.2	11.6	31	55.6%	.212
2021 FS	MIN	MLB	30	2	2	4	57	0	50	41	6	2.6	10.8	60	44.4%	.291
2021 DC	MIN	MLB	30	2	2	4	55	0	56.7	47	7	2.6	10.8	68	44.4%	.291

Comparables: Chris Stratton, Erasmo Ramírez, Jordan Lyles

It was hard for a player to "prove" anything in 2020's condensed campaign, so let's just say that The Doof gave "strong indications" that his 2019 breakout was legitimate. If anything, he might be even a little better now, as Duffey managed to continue missing bats while suddenly turning into a ground ball machine. It's no coincidence that his numbers improved once he mothballed his change and started throwing curves every other pitch. Nobody has ever figured out how to hit his deuce, and by spamming it more often in 2020, hitters were in turn less prepared for the heat—which, in turn, helped it perform better than in years past even as he lost a tick of velocity. While it seems that he's been around forever now, he actually won't be a free agent until after 2023, so Twins fans can expect to see Duffey working in high-leverage situations for years to come.

YEAR	TEAM	LVL	AGE	WHIP	ERA	DRA-	WARP	MPH	FB%	WHF	CSP
2018	ROC	AAA	27	1.15	2.90	88	0.5				
2018	MIN	MLB	27	1.20	7.20	120	-0.1	95.2	61.7%	22.5%	
2019	ROC	AAA	28	0.95	1.32	48	0.5				
2019	MIN	MLB	28	1.01	2.50	62	1.4	95.8	54.0%	33.2%	
2020	MIN	MLB	29	0.79	1.88	71	0.6	94.2	43.8%	36.4%	
2021 FS	MIN	MLB	30	1.13	3.09	76	0.9	95.2	51.7%	32.9%	45.9%
2021 DC	MIN	MLB	30	1.13	3.09	76	1.0	95.2	51.7%	32.9%	45.9%

Tyler Duffey, continued

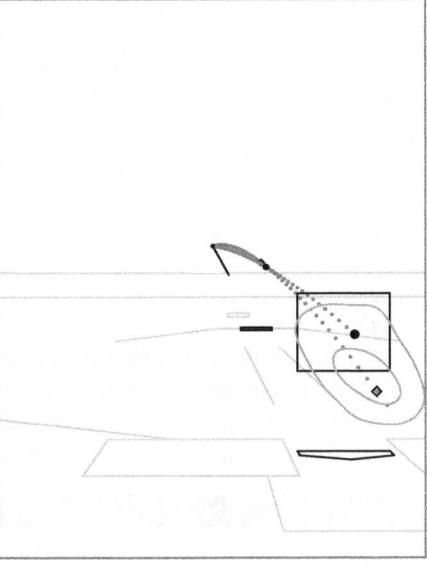

Type	Frequency	Velocity	H Movement	V Movement
● Fastball	41.8%	92.7 [100]	-6.2 [103]	-14.4 [102]
◇ Curveball	56.3%	82.9 [117]	2.7 [80]	-43.8 [110]

J.A. Happ LHP

Born: 10/19/82   Age: 38   Bats: L   Throws: L
Height: 6'5"   Weight: 205   Origin: Round 3, 2004 Draft (#92 overall)

YEAR	TEAM	LVL	AGE	W	L	SV	G	GS	IP	H	HR	BB/9	K/9	K	GB%	BABIP
2018	NYY	MLB	35	7	0	0	11	11	63^2	51	10	2.3	8.9	63	32.2%	.252
2018	TOR	MLB	35	10	6	0	20	20	114	99	17	2.8	10.3	130	44.6%	.286
2019	NYY	MLB	36	12	8	0	31	30	161^1	160	34	2.7	7.8	140	40.5%	.281
2020	NYY	MLB	37	2	2	0	9	9	49^1	37	8	2.7	7.7	42	43.8%	.227
2021 FS	MIN	MLB	38	9	8	0	26	26	150	141	22	3.1	8.3	139	41.7%	.284
2021 DC	MIN	MLB	38	9	8	0	25	25	142.3	134	20	3.1	8.3	132	41.7%	.284

Comparables: Jorge De La Rosa, Kyle Lohse, Todd Stottlemyre

For a guy who was viewed as a bust a few years ago, or as a failure who would never live up to his stellar rookie campaign, it's been an achievement for Happ to grind his way to a serviceable career as a back-end starter well into his late 30s. Did you know that he's one of only 13 pitchers since 2015 with at least 900 innings pitched and an ERA lower than 3.75? That tidbit speaks more to the dwindling role of the starting pitcher in modern baseball than to any greatness on Happ's part, but that kind of reliability makes things easier for any manager, even if it never makes the pitcher in question appointment viewing.

YEAR	TEAM	LVL	AGE	WHIP	ERA	DRA-	WARP	MPH	FB%	WHF	CSP
2018	NYY	MLB	35	1.05	2.69	89	1.0	94.0	72.2%	22.7%	
2018	TOR	MLB	35	1.18	4.18	86	1.9	94.5	74.2%	24.9%	
2019	NYY	MLB	36	1.30	4.91	123	-0.4	93.5	68.3%	23.8%	
2020	NYY	MLB	37	1.05	3.47	105	0.3	93.1	67.1%	22.7%	
2021 FS	MIN	MLB	38	1.29	3.97	95	1.9	93.7	69.5%	23.6%	47.4%
2021 DC	MIN	MLB	38	1.29	3.97	95	1.8	93.7	69.5%	23.6%	47.4%

J.A. Happ, continued

Pitch Shape vs LHH

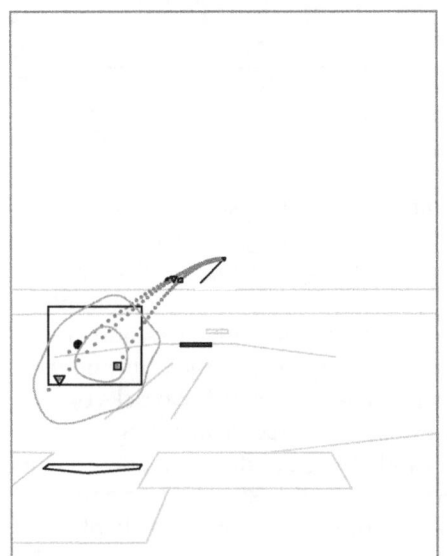

Pitch Shape vs RHH

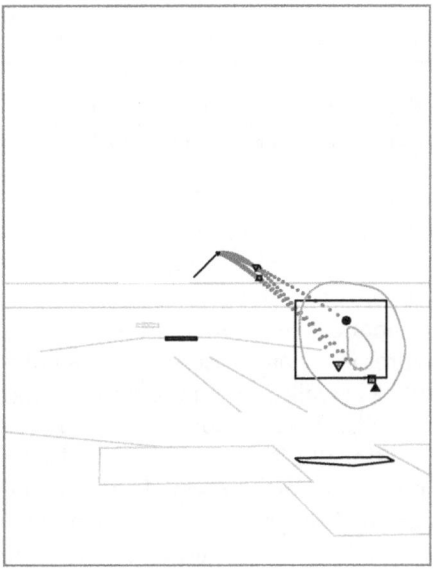

Type	Frequency	Velocity	H Movement	V Movement
● Fastball	44.5%	91.7 [97]	7 [99]	-13.7 [104]
□ Sinker	22.6%	89.3 [84]	12 [108]	-23 [92]
▲ Changeup	13.1%	86.4 [105]	13.5 [91]	-25 [107]
▽ Slider	19.7%	84.1 [101]	-2.4 [89]	-30.7 [109]

Rich Hill LHP

Born: 03/11/80 Age: 41 Bats: L Throws: L
Height: 6'5" Weight: 221 Origin: Round 4, 2002 Draft (#112 overall)

YEAR	TEAM	LVL	AGE	W	L	SV	G	GS	IP	H	HR	BB/9	K/9	K	GB%	BABIP
2018	LAD	MLB	38	11	5	0	25	24	132²	108	20	2.8	10.2	150	37.9%	.272
2019	LAD	MLB	39	4	1	0	13	13	58²	48	10	2.8	11.0	72	47.3%	.284
2020	MIN	MLB	40	2	2	0	8	8	38²	28	3	4.0	7.2	31	41.1%	.240
2021 FS	MIN	MLB	41	10	7	0	26	26	150	132	19	3.2	9.6	159	43.0%	.289
2021 DC	MIN	MLB	41	4	4	0	14	14	72.7	64	9	3.2	9.6	77	43.0%	.289

Comparables: Tom Gordon, LaTroy Hawkins, Dennis Eckersley

History has not been kind to those predicting Hill's demise. He's had Steve Blass disease and Tommy John surgery, suffered the indignity of a demotion from the Trembley-era Orioles, battled approximately a thousand blisters and yet here he is, still getting outs at the age of 40. So, with no small amount of trepidation: Hill looks like he's really slowing down. His sparkly ERA and FIP figures from last season are undercut by an alarming dip in strikeouts and uptick in walks. Under the hood, things look no better. He lost two ticks on his fastball, and his famously invincible curve wasn't quite so devastating. Traditionally, it's a pitch that steals strikes, induces grounders and draws a fair amount of whiffs to boot. Last year, hitters swung and missed far less and started hitting it in the air more often. A suspiciously low homer rate kept everything glued together, but that won't hold unless his velocity comes back. All told, he's the old man of the league, his stuff is in decline and he hasn't managed to average even five innings per start since 2018. He'll deservedly get another chance in 2021, but at long last, the end appears nigh.

YEAR	TEAM	LVL	AGE	WHIP	ERA	DRA-	WARP	MPH	FB%	WHF	CSP
2018	LAD	MLB	38	1.12	3.66	87	2.1	91.2	58.8%	24.8%	
2019	LAD	MLB	39	1.12	2.45	69	1.5	92.2	52.6%	26.0%	
2020	MIN	MLB	40	1.16	3.03	119	0.0	89.7	46.8%	16.0%	
2021 FS	MIN	MLB	41	1.24	3.71	86	2.6	91.1	53.0%	22.4%	53.7%
2021 DC	MIN	MLB	41	1.24	3.71	86	1.3	91.1	53.0%	22.4%	53.7%

Rich Hill, continued

Pitch Shape vs LHH

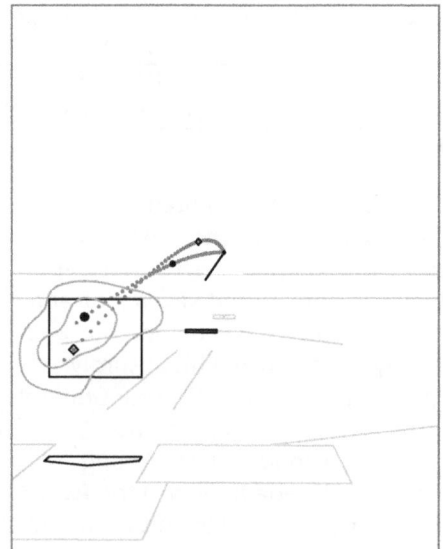

Pitch Shape vs RHH

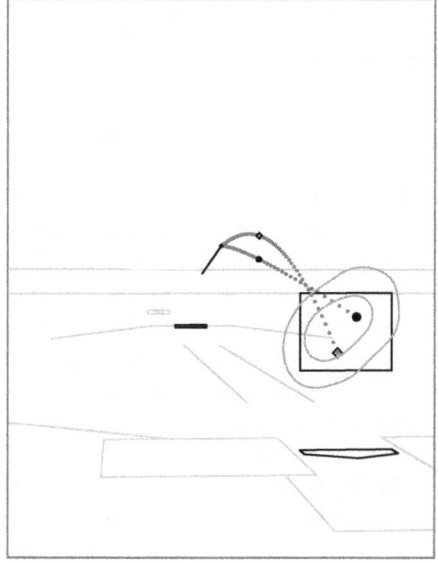

Type	Frequency	Velocity	H Movement	V Movement
● Fastball	44.1%	87.9 [85]	8.8 [90]	-15 [101]
+ Cutter	3.6%	83.3 [68]	-3.1 [108]	-28.5 [83]
◇ Curveball	49.1%	72.5 [76]	-17.2 [139]	-58.9 [77]

Kenta Maeda RHP

Born: 04/11/88 Age: 33 Bats: R Throws: R
Height: 6'1" Weight: 185 Origin: International Free Agent, 2016

YEAR	TEAM	LVL	AGE	W	L	SV	G	GS	IP	H	HR	BB/9	K/9	K	GB%	BABIP
2018	LAD	MLB	30	8	10	2	39	20	125^1	115	13	3.1	11.0	153	39.9%	.323
2019	LAD	MLB	31	10	8	3	37	26	153^2	114	22	3.0	9.9	169	39.5%	.245
2020	MIN	MLB	32	6	1	0	11	11	66^2	40	9	1.4	10.8	80	47.5%	.208
2021 FS	MIN	MLB	33	10	6	0	26	26	150	119	16	2.5	10.4	172	43.8%	.278
2021 DC	MIN	MLB	33	11	6	0	27	27	156.7	124	17	2.5	10.4	180	43.8%	.278

Comparables: Carlos Carrasco, Jacob deGrom, Corey Kluber

    The idea that a player can be "underrated" is a fraught and tired concept, but Maeda never really received his due as one of the better pitchers in baseball during his Dodgers days. For all their success and competence, Los Angeles never quite seemed to appreciate what they had here. Despite averaging about four WARP per season, the Dodgers shuttled Maeda between the rotation and bullpen throughout his time in town, and they dealt him and his absurdly affordable contract to Minnesota for bullpen help last winter. Brusdar Graterol was a fine pick-up, of course, but even the best of relievers look a little underwhelming compared to a guy who finished second in the Cy Young balloting. Given a permanent spot in the rotation, Maeda thrived in the Twin Cities. He led the league in WHIP, struck out nearly a third of the hitters he faced and finally saw his ERA catch up to his peripherals. He may not be the second best pitcher in the AL going forward, but it should come as no surprise if he's in the top 10 or 15. It's familiar turf for him, after all.

YEAR	TEAM	LVL	AGE	WHIP	ERA	DRA-	WARP	MPH	FB%	WHF	CSP
2018	LAD	MLB	30	1.26	3.81	62	3.6	93.5	44.4%	31.8%	
2019	LAD	MLB	31	1.07	4.04	67	4.1	93.9	37.3%	32.6%	
2020	MIN	MLB	32	0.75	2.70	74	1.5	93.5	25.9%	34.8%	
2021 FS	MIN	MLB	33	1.08	2.65	67	4.2	93.7	35.3%	33.1%	45.1%
2021 DC	MIN	MLB	33	1.08	2.65	67	4.3	93.7	35.3%	33.1%	45.1%

Kenta Maeda, continued

Pitch Shape vs LHH

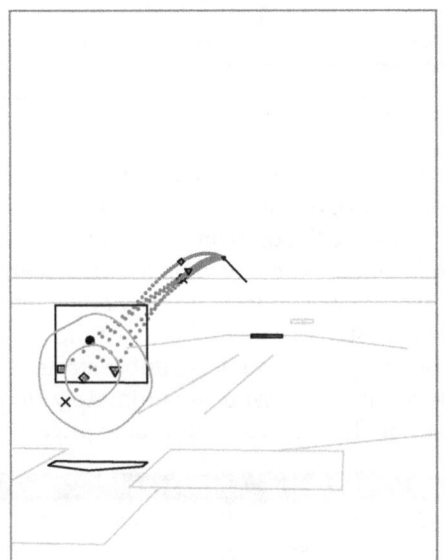

Pitch Shape vs RHH

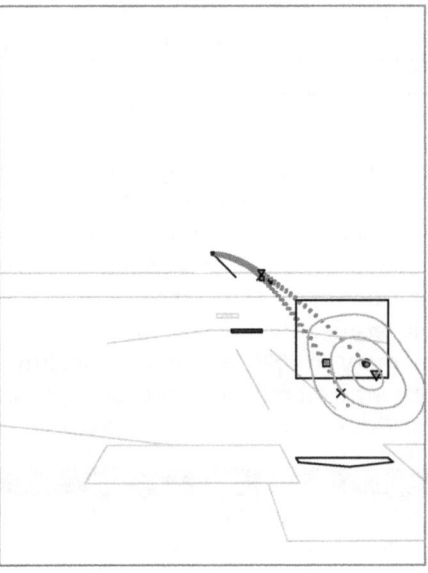

Type	Frequency	Velocity	H Movement	V Movement
● Fastball	19.0%	91.8 [97]	-6.9 [99]	-15.4 [100]
□ Sinker	6.9%	90.9 [92]	-14.3 [91]	-21.8 [96]
✕ Splitter	29.3%	84.6 [97]	-11.2 [88]	-32 [91]
▽ Slider	39.6%	83.1 [96]	2.9 [91]	-29.8 [111]
◇ Curveball	3.3%	78.4 [99]	6.2 [95]	-47.5 [102]

Jake Odorizzi RHP

Born: 03/27/90 Age: 31 Bats: R Throws: R
Height: 6'2" Weight: 190 Origin: Round 1, 2008 Draft (#32 overall)

YEAR	TEAM	LVL	AGE	W	L	SV	G	GS	IP	H	HR	BB/9	K/9	K	GB%	BABIP
2018	MIN	MLB	28	7	10	0	32	32	164^1	151	20	3.8	8.9	162	28.2%	.293
2019	MIN	MLB	29	15	7	0	30	30	159	139	16	3.0	10.1	178	34.3%	.305
2020	MIN	MLB	30	0	1	0	4	4	13^2	16	4	2.0	7.9	12	34.9%	.308
2021 FS	MIN	MLB	31	9	8	0	26	26	150	132	23	3.7	9.2	154	35.0%	.275

Comparables: Ervin Santana, Nathan Eovaldi, Anthony DeSclafani

Odorizzi took a qualifying offer in lieu of hitting free agency last winter. That choice seemed reasonable back then but aged like an investment in downtown real estate. The long-dormant hot stove sparked to life days after the right-hander pledged to stay with the Twins, so instead of cashing in on a career year, he'll now have to test the waters in a market that will almost certainly be far less player-friendly. To make matters worse, his All-Star 2019 feels like a distant memory. In 2020, he was only healthy enough to make four forgettable starts, playing a bit role on Minnesota's division-winning club. Whoever ultimately wins the Odorizzi stands to pick up a pretty good pitcher at a very affordable price.

YEAR	TEAM	LVL	AGE	WHIP	ERA	DRA-	WARP	MPH	FB%	WHF	CSP
2018	MIN	MLB	28	1.34	4.49	125	-0.6	92.9	54.3%	24.8%	
2019	MIN	MLB	29	1.21	3.51	86	2.7	94.3	57.8%	27.9%	
2020	MIN	MLB	30	1.39	6.59	117	0.0	94.1	41.8%	19.9%	
2021 FS	MIN	MLB	31	1.29	4.02	96	1.8	93.9	55.2%	26.2%	44.3%

Jake Odorizzi, continued

Pitch Shape vs LHH

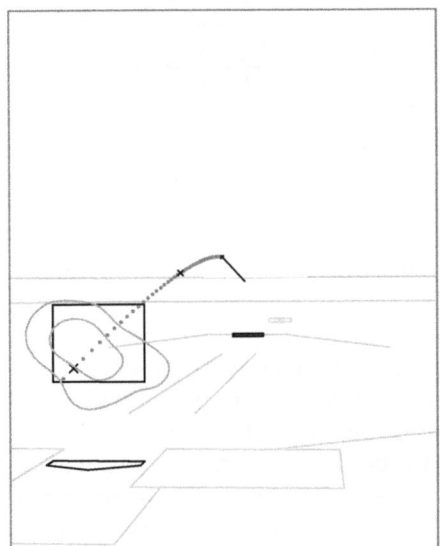

Pitch Shape vs RHH

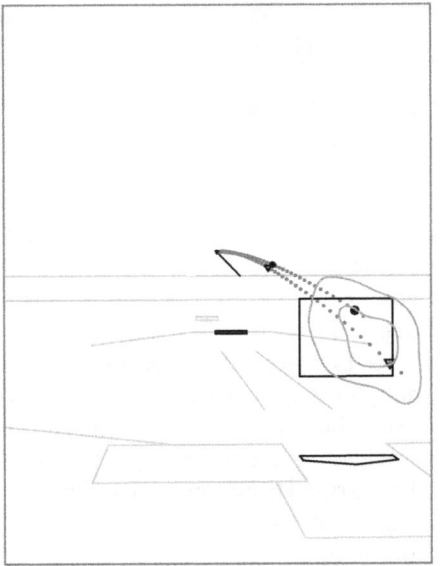

Type	Frequency	Velocity	H Movement	V Movement
● Fastball	29.6%	93.1 [102]	-8.7 [90]	-13.4 [105]
□ Sinker	12.1%	93.1 [104]	-12 [107]	-16.1 [114]
+ Cutter	11.1%	88.8 [103]	1.6 [98]	-20.7 [114]
✕ Splitter	23.6%	85 [99]	-8.6 [97]	-30 [98]
▽ Slider	18.2%	84.6 [103]	5.1 [99]	-30.9 [108]
◇ Curveball	5.4%	75.2 [86]	6.7 [97]	-51.5 [93]

Michael Pineda   RHP
Born: 01/18/89   Age: 32   Bats: R   Throws: R
Height: 6'7"   Weight: 280   Origin: International Free Agent, 2005

YEAR	TEAM	LVL	AGE	W	L	SV	G	GS	IP	H	HR	BB/9	K/9	K	GB%	BABIP
2018	FTM	HI-A	29	0	0	0	2	2	6	7	0	0.0	6.0	4	35.0%	.350
2019	MIN	MLB	30	11	5	0	26	26	146	141	23	1.7	8.6	140	35.1%	.294
2020	MIN	MLB	31	2	0	0	5	5	26²	25	0	2.4	8.4	25	37.2%	.321
2021 FS	MIN	MLB	32	9	8	0	26	26	150	145	22	2.3	8.6	143	39.3%	.295
2021 DC	MIN	MLB	32	8	7	0	24	24	131	127	19	2.3	8.6	125	39.3%	.295

Comparables: Masahiro Tanaka, Stephen Strasburg, Ricky Nolasco

    Pineda has lived a full baseball life. A top prospect, he burst onto the scene as a rookie flamethrower, earning an All-Star nod in his first season. He was then dealt to the sport's most historic franchise in a blockbuster deal, only to miss two seasons with shoulder problems. Since then, he hasn't always been great, but he sure has been notable: Rotation savior, pine-tar user, strikeout rate leader, booed out of the Bronx, missed another year on the shelf and, finally, emerged on the other side as a dependable starter in Minnesota. Last season, he channeled the home-run suppressing form of the earliest days of his career, as he was the only pitcher in 2020 to start multiple games and not allow a home run. He no longer resembles the flamethrower he was in his youth, but as he's matured, he's learned how to work off of his slider and change. Pineda's a better pitcher for it, and a reminder that, for starters especially, velocity isn't everything.

YEAR	TEAM	LVL	AGE	WHIP	ERA	DRA-	WARP	MPH	FB%	WHF	CSP
2018	FTM	HI-A	29	1.17	1.50	83	0.1				
2019	MIN	MLB	30	1.16	4.01	97	1.6	94.8	55.5%	25.7%	
2020	MIN	MLB	31	1.20	3.38	86	0.4	94.1	50.1%	29.3%	
2021 FS	MIN	MLB	32	1.23	3.85	93	2.0	94.7	54.3%	26.5%	49.0%
2021 DC	MIN	MLB	32	1.23	3.85	93	1.8	94.7	54.3%	26.5%	49.0%

Michael Pineda, continued

Pitch Shape vs LHH

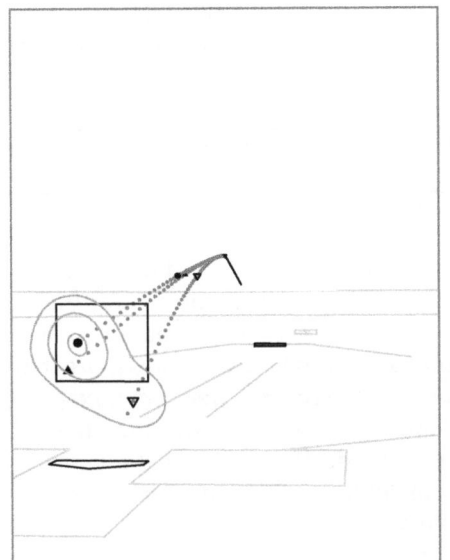

Pitch Shape vs RHH

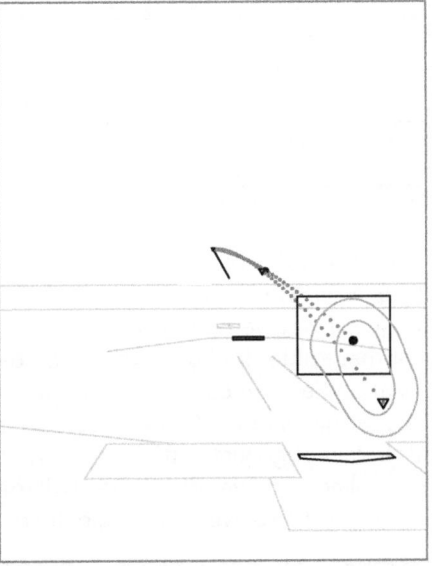

Type	Frequency	Velocity	H Movement	V Movement
● Fastball	50.1%	92.1 [99]	-6.3 [102]	-15.8 [98]
▲ Changeup	11.4%	85.7 [102]	-14.5 [85]	-27 [101]
▽ Slider	38.5%	82.5 [94]	0.5 [82]	-35.9 [94]

Hansel Robles   RHP

Born: 08/13/90   Age: 30   Bats: R   Throws: R
Height: 6'0"   Weight: 220   Origin: International Free Agent, 2008

YEAR	TEAM	LVL	AGE	W	L	SV	G	GS	IP	H	HR	BB/9	K/9	K	GB%	BABIP
2018	LV	AAA	27	0	0	2	8	0	7^2	7	1	5.9	8.2	7	60.9%	.273
2018	NYM	MLB	27	2	2	0	16	0	19^2	21	7	4.6	10.5	23	25.9%	.304
2018	LAA	MLB	27	0	1	2	37	0	36^1	32	2	3.7	8.9	36	39.2%	.303
2019	LAA	MLB	28	5	1	23	71	1	72^2	58	6	2.0	9.3	75	38.0%	.283
2020	LAA	MLB	29	0	2	1	18	0	16^2	19	4	5.4	10.8	20	32.7%	.341
2021 FS	MIN	MLB	30	2	2	0	57	0	50	44	7	3.9	9.6	53	36.0%	.285
2021 DC	MIN	MLB	30	2	2	0	55	0	56.7	50	8	3.9	9.6	60	36.0%	.285

Comparables: Shawn Armstrong, Evan Marshall, Nick Wittgren

Robles took a big step back after being one of the league's best relievers in 2019, as his walk and home run rates overcorrected from his career year. But frankly, if you weren't expecting this, the "fool me twice" rule comes into effect. Not that Robles had been that good before, but his control vacillates more than a Mariah Carey vocal range showcase. In terms of lyrics, the newly minted 30-year-old is more Vampire Weekend: "Nobody knows what the future holds / It's bad enough just getting old." On the wrong side of the age hill, the Twins, who inked him over the winter, will tolerate Robles' inconsistency less and less moving forward even if the velocity recovers.

YEAR	TEAM	LVL	AGE	WHIP	ERA	DRA-	WARP	MPH	FB%	WHF	CSP
2018	LV	AAA	27	1.57	3.52	104	0.0				
2018	NYM	MLB	27	1.58	5.03	83	0.3	97.3	69.0%	25.5%	
2018	LAA	MLB	27	1.29	2.97	109	0.0	98.7	67.5%	27.3%	
2019	LAA	MLB	28	1.02	2.48	75	1.3	99.0	56.3%	26.9%	
2020	LAA	MLB	29	1.74	10.26	108	0.1	97.6	52.1%	30.7%	
2021 FS	MIN	MLB	30	1.32	4.07	95	0.4	98.6	58.0%	27.7%	49.3%
2021 DC	MIN	MLB	30	1.32	4.07	95	0.4	98.6	58.0%	27.7%	49.3%

Hansel Robles, continued

Pitch Shape vs LHH	Pitch Shape vs RHH
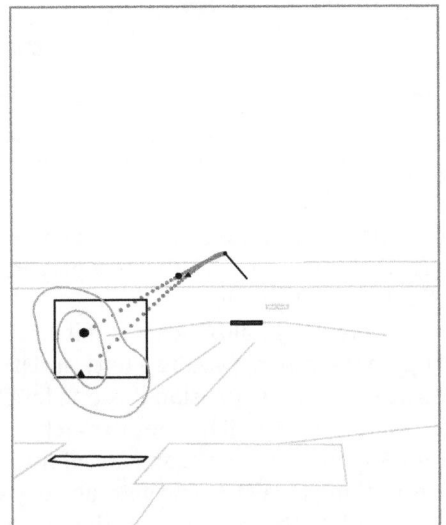	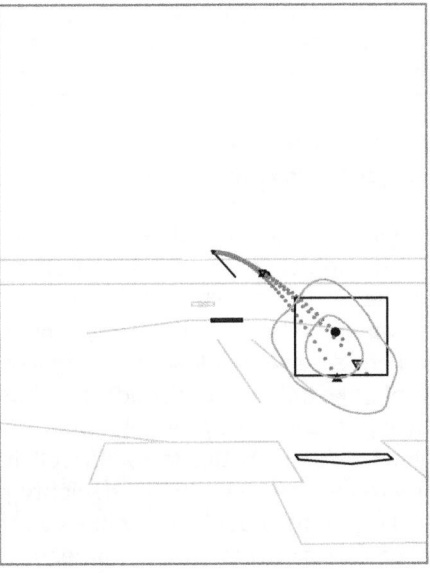

Type	Frequency	Velocity	H Movement	V Movement
● Fastball	51.7%	95.5 [109]	-11.1 [79]	-12.5 [107]
▲ Changeup	36.0%	88.1 [112]	-13 [93]	-26.8 [102]
▽ Slider	12.0%	88.9 [122]	-1.2 [76]	-26.6 [121]

Sergio Romo   RHP

Born: 03/04/83   Age: 38   Bats: R   Throws: R
Height: 5'11"   Weight: 185   Origin: Round 28, 2005 Draft (#852 overall)

YEAR	TEAM	LVL	AGE	W	L	SV	G	GS	IP	H	HR	BB/9	K/9	K	GB%	BABIP
2018	TB	MLB	35	3	4	25	73	5	67^1	65	11	2.7	10.0	75	36.6%	.312
2019	MIA	MLB	36	2	0	17	38	0	37^2	33	4	3.1	7.9	33	36.4%	.274
2019	MIN	MLB	36	0	1	3	27	0	22^2	17	3	1.6	10.7	27	35.0%	.246
2020	MIN	MLB	37	1	2	5	24	0	20	16	3	3.1	10.3	23	31.5%	.255
2021 FS	MIN	MLB	38	2	2	3	57	0	50	44	7	2.7	9.2	51	35.7%	.279
2021 DC	MIN	MLB	38	2	2	3	55	0	48	42	6	2.7	9.2	49	35.7%	.279

Comparables: Trevor Hoffman, Tom Henke, Rafael Betancourt

Like an ultimate frisbee player vainly chasing a disc, batters are still reaching for Romo's slider and catching nothing but air. You would think the best players in the world would have cracked this particular case by now: Romo's only weapon is a long but relatively slow sweeping breaking ball. Odds are, if it starts on one side of the plate, it's going to end up on the other. If you're a lefty and it looks like it'll fly over the adjacent batter's box, dust off your "slap this one foul" swing, because it's probably coming in the back door. And if he tries to catch you flat-footed with a fastball...well, it's only 85 mph these days and, as all the Twitter experts have decided, eighty-poo is nothing to sweat. The veteran keeps ticking along though, and while you could speculate that a slight velo downtick is cause for concern, we're not ready to do so. Father Time comes for 'em all eventually, but Romo struck out more than 10 per nine, suggesting he still has another year or two in the tank.

YEAR	TEAM	LVL	AGE	WHIP	ERA	DRA-	WARP	MPH	FB%	WHF	CSP
2018	TB	MLB	35	1.26	4.14	62	1.7	87.7	30.1%	31.9%	
2019	MIA	MLB	36	1.22	3.58	118	-0.2	87.4	26.2%	30.1%	
2019	MIN	MLB	36	0.93	3.18	55	0.6	87.3	22.0%	30.6%	
2020	MIN	MLB	37	1.15	4.05	109	0.1	86.7	25.8%	28.6%	
2021 FS	MIN	MLB	38	1.18	3.43	85	0.7	87.3	26.3%	30.3%	42.5%
2021 DC	MIN	MLB	38	1.18	3.43	85	0.6	87.3	26.3%	30.3%	42.5%

Sergio Romo, continued

Pitch Shape vs LHH

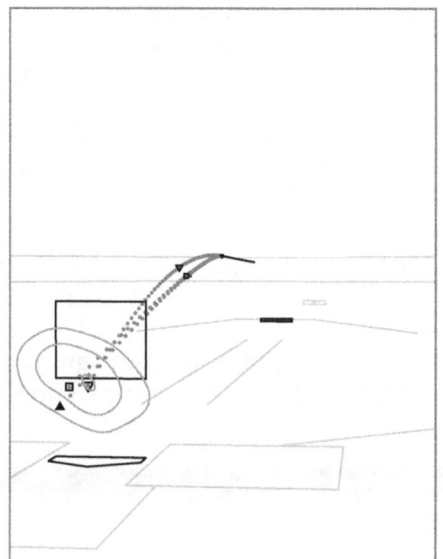

Pitch Shape vs RHH

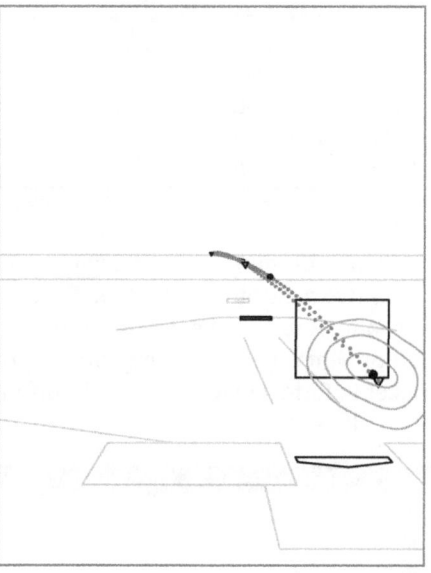

Type	Frequency	Velocity	H Movement	V Movement
● Fastball	12.1%	86 [79]	-12.7 [71]	-22.5 [79]
□ Sinker	13.7%	84.7 [60]	-17.1 [70]	-30.5 [68]
▲ Changeup	9.6%	79.9 [80]	-17.6 [69]	-35 [79]
▽ Slider	64.6%	76.1 [65]	14.1 [134]	-36.1 [93]

Minnesota Twins 2021

Cody Stashak RHP
Born: 06/04/94 Age: 27 Bats: R Throws: R
Height: 6'2" Weight: 180 Origin: Round 13, 2015 Draft (#380 overall)

YEAR	TEAM	LVL	AGE	W	L	SV	G	GS	IP	H	HR	BB/9	K/9	K	GB%	BABIP
2018	CHA	AA	24	1	1	4	35	2	55^2	47	4	2.1	11.2	69	31.2%	.321
2019	PNS	AA	25	2	3	4	19	0	28^1	28	4	1.6	12.7	40	27.4%	.353
2019	ROC	AAA	25	5	0	0	14	2	25	17	1	1.4	12.2	34	40.7%	.276
2019	MIN	MLB	25	0	1	0	18	1	25	29	3	0.4	9.0	25	24.7%	.351
2020	MIN	MLB	26	1	0	0	11	0	15	11	2	1.8	10.2	17	37.8%	.257
2021 FS	MIN	MLB	27	2	2	0	57	0	50	44	8	2.6	10.2	56	32.1%	.288
2021 DC	MIN	MLB	27	2	2	0	55	0	51	45	8	2.6	10.2	57	32.1%	.288

Comparables: Jonathan Holder, Erick Fedde, Wes Parsons

    A scoop of mint chip in a sugar cone. A 2004 Honda Accord. An empty parking space two aisles from the door. Blue Moon. A Lyft ride with a driver who sprayed only one bottle of Axe in their Prius. The Arizona State Sun Devils football team. Junior Mints. The Cars. Sixty-one degrees with the sun just poking through. Ticket to Ride. Movie theaters. Kauffman Stadium. A 25-minute bike ride. Cody Stashak.

YEAR	TEAM	LVL	AGE	WHIP	ERA	DRA-	WARP	MPH	FB%	WHF	CSP
2018	CHA	AA	24	1.08	2.75	68	1.2				
2019	PNS	AA	25	1.16	4.76	107	-0.2				
2019	ROC	AAA	25	0.84	1.44	47	1.0				
2019	MIN	MLB	25	1.20	3.24	119	-0.1	93.0	54.0%	31.1%	
2020	MIN	MLB	26	0.93	3.00	89	0.2	93.1	55.1%	29.9%	
2021 FS	MIN	MLB	27	1.19	3.76	91	0.5	93.1	54.5%	30.5%	48.9%
2021 DC	MIN	MLB	27	1.19	3.76	91	0.5	93.1	54.5%	30.5%	48.9%

Cody Stashak, continued

Pitch Shape vs LHH

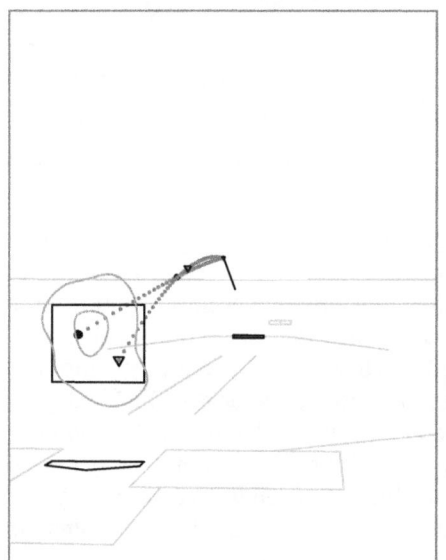

Pitch Shape vs RHH

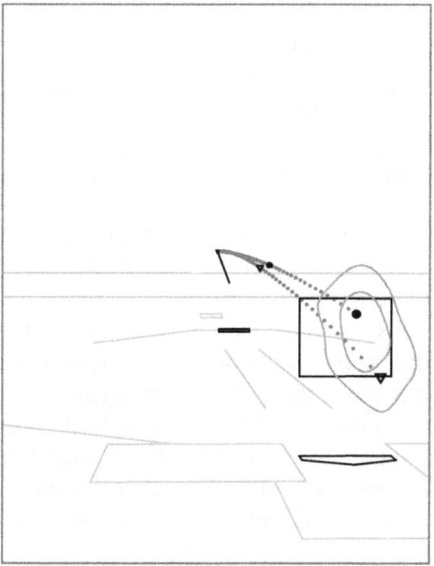

Type	Frequency	Velocity	H Movement	V Movement
● Fastball	55.1%	92 [98]	-5.8 [104]	-12 [109]
▲ Changeup	4.0%	86.1 [104]	-11.3 [102]	-24.2 [109]
▽ Slider	41.0%	82.2 [92]	7.9 [110]	-31.4 [107]

Minnesota Twins 2021

Caleb Thielbar LHP
Born: 01/31/87   Age: 34   Bats: R   Throws: L
Height: 6'0"   Weight: 205   Origin: Round 18, 2009 Draft (#556 overall)

YEAR	TEAM	LVL	AGE	W	L	SV	G	GS	IP	H	HR	BB/9	K/9	K	GB%	BABIP
2018	ERI	AA	31	3	0	0	27	0	38	28	1	0.7	9.5	40	35.6%	.273
2018	TOL	AAA	31	4	1	0	12	0	19	20	2	0.9	5.2	11	38.1%	.295
2019	TOL	AAA	32	2	1	4	50	0	76^1	74	7	1.9	10.8	92	38.1%	.345
2020	MIN	MLB	33	2	1	0	17	0	20	14	0	4.0	9.9	22	27.5%	.275
2021 FS	MIN	MLB	34	2	2	0	57	0	50	45	7	2.9	9.1	50	36.3%	.287
2021 DC	MIN	MLB	34	2	2	0	55	0	51	46	7	2.9	9.1	52	36.3%	.287

Comparables: Sam Freeman, Javy Guerra, Ryan Buchter

While it's not quite as improbable as Daniel Bard's comeback in Colorado, Thielbar's return from the wilderness is a great story in its own right. After years of injuries and bus rides and Triple-A hotels, the lefty finally called it quits after 2019 and took a job as Augustana University's pitching coach. It proved to be a quick stint on campus. Minnesota coaxed him to Fort Myers to give the mound one more shot, which proved an excellent decision for all parties, as Thielbar recaptured his 2013-14 form and emerged as a solid contributor in the Twins bullpen. He's not quite a late-inning guy— his lone hold came in the sixth inning— but regardless of his ultimate role, his ascension from D-II coach to major league reliever is one of the better things to come out of 2020—unless you pitch for the Vikings, perhaps.

YEAR	TEAM	LVL	AGE	WHIP	ERA	DRA-	WARP	MPH	FB%	WHF	CSP
2018	ERI	AA	31	0.82	1.42	70	0.7				
2018	TOL	AAA	31	1.16	3.32	73	0.3				
2019	TOL	AAA	32	1.18	3.30	72	2.0				
2020	MIN	MLB	33	1.15	2.25	97	0.2	92.1	54.4%	29.4%	
2021 FS	MIN	MLB	34	1.23	3.76	90	0.5	92.1	54.4%	29.4%	50.7%
2021 DC	MIN	MLB	34	1.23	3.76	90	0.5	92.1	54.4%	29.4%	50.7%

Caleb Thielbar, continued

Pitch Shape vs LHH

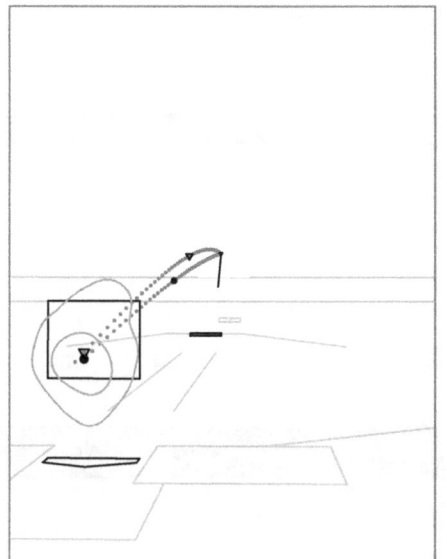

Pitch Shape vs RHH

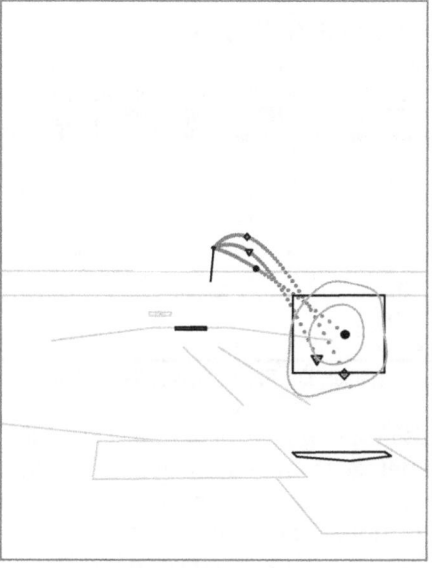

Type	Frequency	Velocity	H Movement	V Movement
● Fastball	54.4%	89.9 [92]	1.4 [125]	-12.9 [107]
▽ Slider	20.2%	77.9 [73]	-12 [126]	-40.6 [80]
◇ Curveball	25.3%	68.8 [62]	-5.9 [93]	-71.2 [49]

PLAYER COMMENTS WITHOUT GRAPHS

Willians Astudillo C
Born: 10/14/91   Age: 29   Bats: R   Throws: R
Height: 5'9"   Weight: 225   Origin: International Free Agent, 2008

YEAR	TEAM	LVL	AGE	PA	R	2B	3B	HR	RBI	BB	K	SB	CS	AVG/OBP/SLG
2018	ROC	AAA	26	307	30	17	1	12	38	10	14	7	4	.276/.314/.469
2018	MIN	MLB	26	97	9	4	1	3	21	2	3	0	0	.355/.371/.516
2019	ROC	AAA	27	83	18	1	0	5	19	2	2	1	1	.423/.446/.628
2019	MIN	MLB	27	204	28	9	0	4	21	5	8	0	0	.268/.299/.379
2020	MIN	MLB	28	16	4	1	0	1	3	0	2	0	0	.250/.250/.500
2021 FS	MIN	MLB	29	600	74	30	1	19	80	19	45	1	1	.289/.328/.455
2021 DC	MIN	MLB	29	62	7	3	0	2	8	2	4	0	0	.289/.328/.455

Comparables: Ken Retzer, Mackey Sasser, Del Rice

It's now been two years since Astudillo emerged from minor-league obscurity. His rectangular frame, bizarre positional flexibility and retrograde knack for contact endeared him to a larger audience than most 26-year-old afterthoughts generally garner. But right when he seemed poised to become a cult hero, a funny thing happened: the Twins suddenly got good. A 90-loss team has the luxury of giving a vaguely promising misfit several hundred at-bats to see if they've unearthed a hidden gem. Contenders don't, and after a cold streak in 2019 and a cup of coffee last season, it's clear that Astudillo is no longer in Minnesota's plans. The indy-ball vibes here are strong, but perhaps a cellar-dweller can find use for him before he fades into the hinterlands.

YEAR	TEAM	P. COUNT	FRM RUNS	BLK RUNS	THRW RUNS	TOT RUNS
2018	MIN	2271	1.1	0.5	0.0	1.6
2018	ROC	5323	1.4	0.3	0.3	1.9
2019	MIN	2577	-0.3	0.0	-0.1	-0.4
2019	ROC	1130	1.5	0.0	0.0	1.4
2020	MIN	595	0.2	0.0	0.0	0.2
2021	MIN	2405	0.6	-0.1	0.2	0.7
2021	MIN	2405	0.6	0.2	0.2	1.0

YEAR	TEAM	LVL	AGE	PA	DRC+	BABIP	BRR	FRAA	WARP
2018	ROC	AAA	26	307	109	.255	-1.4	C(39): 2.5, 3B(28): 0.6, LF(6): 0.8	1.3
2018	MIN	MLB	26	97	128	.341	0.4	C(16): 2.1, 3B(6): -0.0, 2B(2): 0.0	1.0
2019	ROC	AAA	27	83	168	.389	0.6	C(8): 1.3, 3B(5): 0.4, RF(5): -0.6	1.1
2019	MIN	MLB	27	204	94	.258	-2.1	C(21): -0.4, 1B(15): -0.3, 3B(13): -0.5	0.4
2020	MIN	MLB	28	16	95	.231	0.1	C(6): -0.0	0.1
2021 FS	MIN	MLB	29	600	116	.286	-0.9	C 7, 1B 0	3.7
2021 DC	MIN	MLB	29	62	116	.286	-0.1	C 1	0.5

Travis Blankenhorn 2B

Born: 08/03/96 Age: 24 Bats: L Throws: R
Height: 6'2" Weight: 235 Origin: Round 3, 2015 Draft (#80 overall)

YEAR	TEAM	LVL	AGE	PA	R	2B	3B	HR	RBI	BB	K	SB	CS	AVG/OBP/SLG
2018	FTM	HI-A	21	493	52	24	6	11	57	34	127	6	4	.231/.299/.387
2019	FTM	HI-A	22	61	6	4	0	1	3	9	12	0	0	.269/.377/.404
2019	PNS	AA	22	410	50	18	2	18	51	18	93	11	0	.278/.312/.474
2020	MIN	MLB	23	4	0	1	0	0	0	0	0	0	0	.333/.500/.667
2021 FS	MIN	MLB	24	600	72	27	3	20	73	34	188	2	2	.227/.283/.403
2021 DC	MIN	MLB	24	31	3	1	0	1	3	1	9	0	0	.227/.283/.403

Comparables: Tyler Ladendorf, Cavan Biggio, Chad Pinder

While you can accuse Blankenhorn of plenty of defensive shortcomings, his bat is worth its weight in gold. If the Twins can't find a spot for him, rebuilding clubs will be lurking.

YEAR	TEAM	LVL	AGE	PA	DRC+	BABIP	BRR	FRAA	WARP
2018	FTM	HI-A	21	493	89	.297	1.2	2B(58): -12.9, 3B(41): -0.8, LF(4): 0.3	-1.5
2019	FTM	HI-A	22	61	133	.333	-0.3	LF(6): -1.1, 2B(5): -0.3, 3B(2): -0.1	0.2
2019	PNS	AA	22	410	119	.323	2.7	2B(67): 3.2, LF(18): 0.1	2.5
2020	MIN	MLB	23	4	89	.333	0.0	2B(1): -0.2	0.0
2021 FS	MIN	MLB	24	600	86	.304	-0.3	LF -3, 2B 0	0.2
2021 DC	MIN	MLB	24	31	86	.304	0.0	LF 0	0.0

Keoni Cavaco SS

Born: 06/02/01 Age: 20 Bats: R Throws: R
Height: 6'2" Weight: 195 Origin: Round 1, 2019 Draft (#13 overall)

YEAR	TEAM	LVL	AGE	PA	R	2B	3B	HR	RBI	BB	K	SB	CS	AVG/OBP/SLG
2019	TWI	ROK	18	92	9	4	0	1	6	4	35	1	1	.172/.217/.253
2021 FS	MIN	MLB	20	600	37	16	2	8	44	26	276	4	3	.153/.196/.234

Comparables: Niko Goodrum, Kaleb Cowart, Steven Baron

A late growth spurt helped Cavaco blossom plus power and speed as an upperclassman and propelled him into the first round of the 2019 draft. He doesn't have a particularly long track record of elite performance, and while he's now everything you'd want in an athlete, he's also a somewhat volatile prospect and a guy that evaluators wanted to see more of in 2020. So much for that. Time will tell, but Cavaco may be the kind of player most affected by a lost season, a toolsy youngster still growing into his frame who could have really benefited from additional reps against age-appropriate competition.

YEAR	TEAM	LVL	AGE	PA	DRC+	BABIP	BRR	FRAA	WARP
2019	TWI	ROK	18	92		.275			
2021 FS	MIN	MLB	20	600	15	.277	0.3	SS 2	-4.5

Gilberto Celestino CF

Born: 02/13/99   Age: 22   Bats: R   Throws: L
Height: 6'0"   Weight: 170   Origin: International Free Agent, 2015

YEAR	TEAM	LVL	AGE	PA	R	2B	3B	HR	RBI	BB	K	SB	CS	AVG/OBP/SLG
2018	ELZ	ROK	19	117	13	4	1	1	13	6	16	8	2	.266/.308/.349
2018	TRI	SS	19	142	18	8	0	4	21	10	25	14	0	.323/.387/.480
2019	CR	LO-A	20	503	52	24	3	10	51	48	81	14	8	.276/.350/.409
2019	FTM	HI-A	20	33	6	4	0	0	3	2	4	0	0	.300/.333/.433
2021 FS	MIN	MLB	22	600	50	24	2	10	55	36	170	11	4	.217/.269/.329

Comparables: Jake Cave, Domonic Brown, Dalton Pompey

In 2019 Celestino had an encouraging, if not quite jaw-dropping campaign in the Midwest League, which normally would have punched his ticket for High-A the following spring. Instead, with minor league action cancelled, Celestino was deemed sufficiently promising to warrant an assignment to the alternate training site. There, he spent his evenings getting on a first-name basis with St. Paul's DoorDash drivers, and his days facing pitchers who were all some combination of older, better and more experienced than himself. We don't know how he performed. Only Twins personnel can tell us that and they don't really have any incentive to do that for us. As MLB teams scrap their minor-league affiliates, we can bet that we'll see more of this kind of thing: more prospects sent to sink or swim against better and older players. It'll be an interesting experiment: perhaps Celestino's performance going forward will give us some indication of its merits.

YEAR	TEAM	LVL	AGE	PA	DRC+	BABIP	BRR	FRAA	WARP
2018	ELZ	ROK	19	117		.301			
2018	TRI	SS	19	142	167	.374	1.6	CF(16): 0.9, RF(12): 2.6, LF(3): -0.8	1.2
2019	CR	LO-A	20	503	137	.317	-3.6	CF(83): 3.7, RF(25): -3.6	3.0
2019	FTM	HI-A	20	33	124	.333	0.2	CF(4): -0.8, RF(3): -0.3	0.0
2021 FS	MIN	MLB	22	600	65	.291	0.7	CF 6, RF 1	-0.2

Hyun-wook Choi 최형우 OF

Born: 12/04/89 Age: 31 Bats: L Throws: L
Height: 6'0" Weight: 190 Origin:

YEAR	TEAM	LVL	AGE	PA	R	2B	3B	HR	RBI	BB	K	SB	CS	AVG/OBP/SLG
2018	KIA	KBO	28	609	92	34	1	25	103	66	87	3	0	.339/.414/549.000
2019	KIA	KBO	29	555	65	31	1	17	86	85	77	0	1	.300/.413/.485
2020	KIA	KBO	30	600	93	37	1	28	115	70	101	0	0	.354/.433/.590
2021									No projection					

Here we have a lefty who shrugged off a slow start to his career to become the game's best DH and maintain that title throughout his 30s: Who is this, David Ortiz? Ortiz is actually a fair cross-league comparison, as the personable and charismatic Choi is perhaps the game's least well-rounded star. He can't throw, doesn't play the field and he's slower than a tree, but dangit he can hit. His .354 average kept Mel Rojas Jr. from winning the Triple Crown, and he managed to post the league's second best OPS despite playing in a very tough park to hit. While he'll be 37 next year, there's no reason to suspect that Kia's best player has started his descent just yet.

YEAR	TEAM	LVL	AGE	PA	DRC+	BABIP	BRR	FRAA	WARP
2018	KIA	KBO	28	609					
2019	KIA	KBO	29	555					
2020	KIA	KBO	30	600					
2021					No projection				

Minnesota Twins 2021

Josh Donaldson 3B

Born: 12/08/85 Age: 35 Bats: R Throws: R
Height: 6'1" Weight: 210 Origin: Round 1, 2007 Draft (#48 overall)

YEAR	TEAM	LVL	AGE	PA	R	2B	3B	HR	RBI	BB	K	SB	CS	AVG/OBP/SLG
2018	CLE	MLB	32	60	8	3	0	3	7	10	10	0	0	.280/.400/.520
2018	TOR	MLB	32	159	22	11	0	5	16	21	44	2	0	.234/.333/.423
2019	ATL	MLB	33	659	96	33	0	37	94	100	154	4	2	.259/.379/.521
2020	MIN	MLB	34	102	14	2	0	6	11	18	24	0	0	.222/.373/.469
2021 FS	MIN	MLB	35	600	91	25	1	26	78	88	149	4	2	.240/.359/.453
2021 DC	MIN	MLB	35	536	81	22	1	23	70	78	133	4	2	.240/.359/.453

Comparables: Scott Rolen, Matt Carpenter, Howard Johnson

Does Donaldson still have a shot at a Hall-of-Fame career? By traditional standards, the answer is no. Entering his age-35 season, he has barely 1,000 hits to his name. His 225 career homers are nothing to sneeze at, but hardly special for his time. His .272/.369/.508 batting line is impressive but irreparably dampened by the run environment when he first broke out. He has no postseason heroics to fall back upon. He won an MVP, but so did Justin Morneau. Even the sabermetrically savvy will be inclined to glance at his 35 WARP, note that he has a lower JAWS score (top seven seasons of WAR added together) than Evan Longoria, and scroll on to other things. Maybe that's the right approach.

Get a little creative though, and you can make a case.

First, Donaldson may not have the seven elite seasons, but he clearly has five. In that time, playing in the best era for third basemen the game has ever seen, Donaldson reigned. You have to imagine that at least one of Nolan Arenado, Kris Bryant, Manny Machado, Anthony Rendon and Longoria will be inducted someday, and Donaldson was better with the bat than most of them in their primes. He also didn't get a real shot in the big leagues until he was 26. There may have been good reasons for that, but in an era where players generally create most of their value in their early 20s, it's remarkable how good Donaldson has been without getting to play in that time. Moreover, players don't have 20-year careers anymore, and as that trend accelerates, the electorate should strive to induct the players who burned brightest even if they were great for a shorter period of time than stars of previous generations.

Certainly this is all up for debate, and it's reasonable to be intrigued by Donaldson's case and still think he has more work to do to merit the honor. Fortunately for him, he's 35 and still has time to pad his totals. If he ages gracefully, he'll be a tough one for the BBWAA.

YEAR	TEAM	LVL	AGE	PA	DRC+	BABIP	BRR	FRAA	WARP
2018	CLE	MLB	32	60	106	.297	-0.8	3B(12): -0.9	0.1
2018	TOR	MLB	32	159	106	.303	-0.4	3B(26): -0.9, 1B(1): 0.1	0.5
2019	ATL	MLB	33	659	130	.292	-1.0	3B(148): 1.2	5.1
2020	MIN	MLB	34	102	111	.231	0.3	3B(26): -0.4	0.4
2021 FS	MIN	MLB	35	600	129	.286	-0.5	3B -1, 1B 0	3.3
2021 DC	MIN	MLB	35	536	129	.286	-0.5	3B -1	2.9

Nick Gordon SS

Born: 10/24/95   Age: 25   Bats: L   Throws: R
Height: 6'0"   Weight: 160   Origin: Round 1, 2014 Draft (#5 overall)

YEAR	TEAM	LVL	AGE	PA	R	2B	3B	HR	RBI	BB	K	SB	CS	AVG/OBP/SLG
2018	CHA	AA	22	181	22	10	3	5	20	11	27	7	2	.333/.381/.525
2018	ROC	AAA	22	410	40	13	4	2	29	23	82	13	3	.212/.262/.283
2019	ROC	AAA	23	319	49	29	3	4	40	18	65	14	4	.298/.342/.459
2021 FS	MIN	MLB	25	600	62	26	3	9	58	37	158	7	3	.232/.289/.345
2021 DC	MIN	MLB	25	33	3	1	0	0	3	2	8	0	0	.232/.289/.345

Comparables: Orlando Arcia, Darwin Barney, Reid Brignac

At his prospect apex you could dream on Gordon as an everyday middle infielder who could approximate the value, if not quite the shape, of his older brother Dee's career. That ship has sailed.

YEAR	TEAM	LVL	AGE	PA	DRC+	BABIP	BRR	FRAA	WARP
2018	CHA	AA	22	181	139	.366	-1.4	SS(34): 2.4, 2B(6): -0.3	1.2
2018	ROC	AAA	22	410	53	.264	2.8	SS(69): 2.6, 2B(30): 4.1	-0.1
2019	ROC	AAA	23	319	107	.364	-0.1	SS(40): 1.6, 2B(30): -1.4	1.5
2021 FS	MIN	MLB	25	600	75	.309	0.3	2B 2, SS 0	0.1
2021 DC	MIN	MLB	25	33	75	.309	0.0	2B 0	0.0

Wander Javier SS

Born: 12/29/98   Age: 22   Bats: R   Throws: R
Height: 6'1"   Weight: 165   Origin: International Free Agent, 2015

YEAR	TEAM	LVL	AGE	PA	R	2B	3B	HR	RBI	BB	K	SB	CS	AVG/OBP/SLG
2019	CR	LO-A	20	342	43	9	1	11	37	35	116	2	0	.177/.278/.323
2021 FS	MIN	MLB	22	600	46	20	1	10	50	42	238	2	2	.174/.241/.275

Comparables: Yadiel Rivera, Jai Miller, Michael Chavis

Our lead prospect writer, Jeffrey Paternostro, has made a parlor game out of telling readers he has no idea what to expect from Wander Javier. For those reading this space for more insight, we must regrettably refer you back to Jeffrey.

Minnesota Twins 2021

YEAR	TEAM	LVL	AGE	PA	DRC+	BABIP	BRR	FRAA	WARP
2019	CR	LO-A	20	342	69	.243	-0.9	SS(66): 2.0	0.3
2021 FS	MIN	MLB	22	600	41	.282	-0.4	SS 5	-2.2

Alex Kirilloff RF

Born: 11/09/97   Age: 23   Bats: L   Throws: L
Height: 6'2"   Weight: 195   Origin: Round 1, 2016 Draft (#15 overall)

YEAR	TEAM	LVL	AGE	PA	R	2B	3B	HR	RBI	BB	K	SB	CS	AVG/OBP/SLG
2018	CR	LO-A	20	281	36	20	5	13	56	24	47	1	1	.333/.391/.607
2018	FTM	HI-A	20	280	39	24	2	7	45	14	39	3	2	.362/.393/.550
2019	PNS	AA	21	411	47	18	2	9	43	29	76	7	6	.283/.343/.413
2021 FS	MIN	MLB	23	600	69	25	2	17	72	35	143	1	1	.251/.301/.401
2021 DC	MIN	MLB	23	433	50	18	2	12	52	25	103	0	1	.251/.301/.401

Comparables: Brandon Moss, Carlos González, Tyler Austin

Kirilloff became the third player to make his MLB debut in the postseason and the first to record a base hit when he singled against Jose Urquidy. The fact that the Twins felt comfortable thrusting the 22-year-old into the lineup in an elimination game speaks volumes about how they regard Kirilloff. Wrist injuries dampened his numbers in 2019, but when healthy, he has impressive pop and projects to have two plus tools at full maturity. The jury's still out on whether he'll be able to fake it in a corner-outfield spot or have to shift to first base, but his bat is going to carry him regardless of where he ends up.

YEAR	TEAM	LVL	AGE	PA	DRC+	BABIP	BRR	FRAA	WARP
2018	CR	LO-A	20	281	162	.364	-0.8	RF(53): -4.0, CF(0): -0.0	1.5
2018	FTM	HI-A	20	280	162	.399	-0.8	RF(51): 0.4, CF(3): 0.3	1.7
2019	PNS	AA	21	411	120	.333	-3.3	RF(41): -4.0, 1B(35): 0.3, LF(8): -1.0	0.6
2021 FS	MIN	MLB	23	600	90	.309	-0.6	LF -5, RF 0	0.0
2021 DC	MIN	MLB	23	433	90	.309	-0.4	LF -3, RF 0	0.1

Trevor Larnach RF

Born: 02/26/97   Age: 24   Bats: L   Throws: R
Height: 6'4"   Weight: 223   Origin: Round 1, 2018 Draft (#20 overall)

YEAR	TEAM	LVL	AGE	PA	R	2B	3B	HR	RBI	BB	K	SB	CS	AVG/OBP/SLG
2018	ELZ	ROK	21	75	10	5	0	2	16	10	11	2	0	.311/.413/.492
2018	CR	LO-A	21	102	17	8	1	3	10	11	17	1	0	.297/.373/.505
2019	FTM	HI-A	22	361	33	26	1	6	44	35	74	4	1	.316/.382/.459
2019	PNS	AA	22	181	26	4	0	7	22	22	50	0	0	.295/.387/.455
2021 FS	MIN	MLB	24	600	68	24	1	15	66	50	170	0	0	.231/.302/.367
2021 DC	MIN	MLB	24	166	18	6	0	4	18	14	47	0	0	.231/.302/.367

Comparables: Mac Williamson, Preston Tucker, Marcell Ozuna

Larnach's prospect pedigree perhaps deserves more attention, but this one is actually pretty simple: He's a mediocre right fielder but a potential 60/60 bat thanks to a smooth swing, good approach and booming natural power. Whether in 2021 or 2022, Larnach should crack the lineup sooner rather than later.

YEAR	TEAM	LVL	AGE	PA	DRC+	BABIP	BRR	FRAA	WARP
2018	ELZ	ROK	21	75		.340			
2018	CR	LO-A	21	102	149	.338	0.7	RF(17): -1.5	0.5
2019	FTM	HI-A	22	361	165	.389	-1.4	RF(59): -8.1, LF(9): -0.4	1.9
2019	PNS	AA	22	181	146	.390	-0.3	RF(29): -2.2, LF(5): -0.1	0.8
2021 FS	MIN	MLB	24	600	86	.310	-0.8	RF 1, LF 1	0.3
2021 DC	MIN	MLB	24	166	86	.310	-0.2	RF 0, LF 0	0.1

Royce Lewis SS

Born: 06/05/99   Age: 22   Bats: R   Throws: R
Height: 6'2"   Weight: 200   Origin: Round 1, 2017 Draft (#1 overall)

YEAR	TEAM	LVL	AGE	PA	R	2B	3B	HR	RBI	BB	K	SB	CS	AVG/OBP/SLG
2018	CR	LO-A	19	327	50	23	0	9	53	24	49	22	4	.315/.368/.485
2018	FTM	HI-A	19	208	33	6	3	5	21	19	35	6	4	.255/.327/.399
2019	FTM	HI-A	20	418	55	17	3	10	35	27	90	16	8	.238/.289/.376
2019	PNS	AA	20	148	18	9	1	2	14	11	33	6	2	.231/.291/.358
2021 FS	*MIN*	*MLB*	*22*	*600*	*65*	*26*	*2*	*14*	*66*	*40*	*151*	*12*	*5*	*.230/.288/.365*

Comparables: José Rondón, Amed Rosario, Tony Wolters

Lewis is perhaps the most volatile top-tier prospect in baseball. The tools and intangibles that made him the first pick of the draft back in 2017 are mostly intact. He still projects to play a premium position, still looks like he could develop plus game power, still runs really well, still has baseball people raving about his elite makeup. For a kid who reached Double-A as a 20-year-old, everything seems to be pointing in the right direction. And yet, it's hard to shake the impression that Lewis has been trending downward for the better part of the last two years. It started with a disappointing statistical season in 2019. Facing tough competition in a pitcher's league, Lewis endured growing pains in High-A ball, where his approach backed up and he lost some of his feel to hit. Minnesota promoted him to Double-A anyway, and he again struggled, finishing the year with a .290 OBP across both levels. Perhaps more troublingly, the scouting reports matched the numbers. Lewis' swing and hitting mechanics looked uncharacteristically messy, which screwed up his timing and left him off balance against good breaking stuff. And while it still looks like he'll play an important position defensively, it increasingly looks like it won't be short, at least not in the long run. All of this could have been chalked up to a down year if he'd been able to shrug off his slump in 2020 but, of course, there was no 2020 for minor leaguers. Where does that leave us? Lewis is an uber-talented kid, and the kind of guy you'd love to see succeed. He's also two years removed from his last productive season, and while evaluators still like him plenty, there are more whispers about a long developmental path than there were 18 months ago. He wouldn't be the first star to take a step back before bursting forward, and he may be just a mechanical tweak from a reset. Twins fans should hope so, because while Lewis is still a very promising player, he's no longer a "can't-miss" prospect.

YEAR	TEAM	LVL	AGE	PA	DRC+	BABIP	BRR	FRAA	WARP
2018	CR	LO-A	19	327	151	.349	3.7	SS(67): 0.8	3.2
2018	FTM	HI-A	19	208	106	.291	1.7	SS(45): -4.8	0.3
2019	FTM	HI-A	20	418	96	.281	-1.5	SS(84): 4.0	1.8
2019	PNS	AA	20	148	66	.287	2.0	SS(29): -2.6, 2B(1): 0.0, 3B(1): -0.0	0.3
2021 FS	MIN	MLB	22	600	82	.290	0.8	SS 0, CF 0	0.5

Tzu-Wei Lin   2B
Born: 02/15/94   Age: 27   Bats: L   Throws: R
Height: 5'9"   Weight: 180   Origin: International Free Agent, 2012

YEAR	TEAM	LVL	AGE	PA	R	2B	3B	HR	RBI	BB	K	SB	CS	AVG/OBP/SLG
2018	WOR	AAA	24	302	33	20	2	5	25	23	64	3	4	.307/.362/.448
2018	BOS	MLB	24	73	15	6	1	1	6	8	17	0	1	.246/.329/.415
2019	WOR	AAA	25	250	30	11	1	4	22	21	58	6	2	.246/.308/.357
2019	BOS	MLB	25	22	3	2	0	0	1	2	6	1	1	.200/.273/.300
2020	BOS	MLB	26	57	2	1	0	0	3	2	17	0	0	.154/.182/.173
2021 FS	MIN	MLB	27	600	53	27	5	10	57	47	152	5	3	.227/.292/.355

Comparables: Reid Brignac, Ray Olmedo, Ryan Goins

There's no sadder or more succinct way to break down Lin's horrendous 2020 than to point out that he allowed as many runs in his one inning on the mound (three) as he drove in during his 26 games as a hitter.

YEAR	TEAM	LVL	AGE	PA	DRC+	BABIP	BRR	FRAA	WARP
2018	WOR	AAA	24	302	129	.385	-0.4	SS(51): 1.6, CF(9): 0.9, 2B(6): 0.1	2.1
2018	BOS	MLB	24	73	79	.319	0.2	SS(23): -0.3, CF(6): -0.6, 2B(4): 0.0	0.1
2019	WOR	AAA	25	250	84	.311	1.5	SS(27): 4.6, 2B(15): 1.7, LF(6): 1.7	1.2
2019	BOS	MLB	25	22	70	.286	0.0	2B(8): -0.3, SS(2): -0.0, CF(1): -0.0	0.0
2020	BOS	MLB	26	57	61	.222	0.0	SS(12): 0.0, 2B(6): 0.0, LF(4): 0.1	-0.1
2021 FS	MIN	MLB	27	600	75	.298	0.2	SS 2, 2B 0	0.1

Minnesota Twins 2021

Hernán Pérez   2B

Born: 03/26/91   Age: 30   Bats: R   Throws: R
Height: 6'1"   Weight: 213   Origin: International Free Agent, 2007

YEAR	TEAM	LVL	AGE	PA	R	2B	3B	HR	RBI	BB	K	SB	CS	AVG/OBP/SLG
2018	MIL	MLB	27	334	36	11	2	9	29	17	71	11	3	.253/.290/.386
2019	SA	AAA	28	121	18	10	0	5	19	14	23	6	0	.290/.372/.523
2019	MIL	MLB	28	246	29	11	0	8	18	11	66	5	1	.228/.262/.379
2020	CHC	MLB	29	6	0	0	0	0	0	0	2	0	0	.167/.167/.167
2021 FS	MIN	MLB	30	600	61	25	2	20	71	31	145	20	6	.246/.288/.408

Comparables: Pedro Feliz, Charley Smith, Craig Paquette

Pérez's nickname—"Pan Blanco," or, "White Bread"—is appropriate because he's a walking reminder that, like a slice or two of Wonder, some versatile instruments should be left in the pantry when it's time to make a real meal. The Cubs learned that lesson quickly last season, and he appeared in only three games for the big-league team. He'll keep getting jobs until teams realize that just because someone can play everywhere doesn't mean they should play anywhere—except Triple-A, anyway.

YEAR	TEAM	LVL	AGE	PA	DRC+	BABIP	BRR	FRAA	WARP
2018	MIL	MLB	27	334	91	.300	0.6	2B(51): -0.9, RF(27): 0.4, 3B(22): 0.4	0.7
2019	SA	AAA	28	121	126	.329	0.8	1B(10): 1.0, 2B(9): -0.3, 3B(5): 0.5	0.8
2019	MIL	MLB	28	246	68	.283	-1.7	2B(45): 3.4, SS(21): -1.9, 3B(14): 1.2	0.1
2020	CHC	MLB	29	6	72	.250	0.3	1B(2): -0.0, 2B(1): 0.0, LF(1): 0.0	0.0
2021 FS	MIN	MLB	30	600	86	.298	1.7	2B 0, SS -2	0.6

Brent Rooker OF

Born: 11/01/94 Age: 26 Bats: R Throws: R
Height: 6'3" Weight: 225 Origin: Round 1, 2017 Draft (#35 overall)

YEAR	TEAM	LVL	AGE	PA	R	2B	3B	HR	RBI	BB	K	SB	CS	AVG/OBP/SLG
2018	CHA	AA	23	568	72	32	4	22	79	56	150	6	1	.254/.333/.465
2019	TWI	ROK	24	7	2	0	0	0	0	1	0	0	0	.333/.429/.333
2019	ROC	AAA	24	274	41	16	0	14	47	35	95	2	0	.281/.398/.535
2020	MIN	MLB	25	21	4	2	0	1	5	0	5	0	0	.316/.381/.579
2021 FS	MIN	MLB	26	600	66	25	1	18	69	50	207	0	1	.207/.286/.364
2021 DC	MIN	MLB	26	266	29	11	0	8	30	22	91	0	0	.207/.286/.364

Comparables: Travis Demeritte, Matt Clark, Will Craig

Wrist and groin injuries kept Rooker from the majors in 2019 and a global pandemic nearly did the same in 2020. If that wasn't enough, after his belated late-summer debut, he soon succumbed to a broken forearm after getting drilled by a wayward changeup. Upon his return, he'll soon find that the only thing harder than reaching the big city is staying there. The former first-rounder has formidable pop and a promising track record, but he struggles with spin and plays for a team already flush in corner bats. As a 26-year-old right-right type with little defensive value, he won't get many chances and has very little margin for error when they come.

YEAR	TEAM	LVL	AGE	PA	DRC+	BABIP	BRR	FRAA	WARP
2018	CHA	AA	23	568	115	.316	-4.7	1B(47): -5.7, LF(44): -8.2	-1.2
2019	TWI	ROK	24	7		.333			
2019	ROC	AAA	24	274	122	.417	2.6	LF(56): -0.6	1.5
2020	MIN	MLB	25	21	102	.385		RF(4): -0.1, LF(1): -0.1	0.0
2021 FS	MIN	MLB	26	600	81	.295	-0.8	1B -9, LF -1	-1.3
2021 DC	MIN	MLB	26	266	81	.295	-0.4	1B -4, LF 0	-0.7

Minnesota Twins 2021

Aaron Sabato 1B
Born: 06/04/99   Age: 22   Bats: R   Throws: R
Height: 6'2"   Weight: 230   Origin: Round 1, 2020 Draft (#27 overall)

There aren't a lot of right-right first basemen who hear their name called in the first round of the draft, particularly bad-bodied guys with fewer than 400 college at-bats under their belt. In Sabato, the Twins are getting a draft-eligible sophomore who mashed in the ACC. He smacked 25 dingers in 80 games at North Carolina, slugged .700 and posted very encouraging walk and strikeout numbers in his truncated season. That performance in one of college baseball's power conferences made him an interesting target for any front office incorporating college metrics into their evaluation, as Minnesota does. Twins fans will have to hope that those models are on to something, because Sabato is a risky and somewhat divisive prospect. Everyone loves the bat, particularly the power, but first basemen really have to hit to have value, particularly if they're like Sabato and don't offer anything special at the cold corner. This seems like the kind of pick we'll be able to judge relatively quickly: Three years from now, he'll either be in the middle of the order, or Minnesota will want a mulligan.

Alerick Soularie OF
Born: 07/05/99   Age: 22   Bats: R   Throws: R
Height: 6'0"   Weight: 175   Origin: Round 2, 2020 Draft (#59 overall)

Soularie was Minnesota's second-round pick, a center fielder out of Tennessee who signed for $900,000. A good hitter with an excellent eye and feel for hard contact to all fields, he is a skills-over-tools kind of prospect. He's not especially physical nor particularly fast. He also has kind of an awkward swing and few evaluators expect him to stay in center. Most scouts see him as a tweener with a chance to start if he grows into more power, and the consensus is that the Twins reached here. Still, guys who can get the fat part of the bat on the ball like this don't grow on trees, and Soularie did put up good numbers in a very tough college league. It's a bat you can dream on, even if the pick seems a tad underwhelming.

Homer Bailey   RHP

Born: 05/03/86   Age: 35   Bats: R   Throws: R
Height: 6'4"   Weight: 223   Origin: Round 1, 2004 Draft (#7 overall)

YEAR	TEAM	LVL	AGE	W	L	SV	G	GS	IP	H	HR	BB/9	K/9	K	GB%	BABIP
2018	LOU	AAA	32	2	2	0	7	6	37[2]	41	4	2.4	6.7	28	35.8%	.314
2018	CIN	MLB	32	1	14	0	20	20	106[1]	141	23	2.8	6.3	75	41.9%	.331
2019	KC	MLB	33	7	6	0	18	18	90	89	12	3.8	8.1	81	45.9%	.302
2019	OAK	MLB	33	6	3	0	13	13	73[1]	73	9	1.8	8.3	68	42.8%	.302
2020	MIN	MLB	34	1	0	0	2	2	8	6	1	3.4	7.9	7	36.4%	.238
2021 FS	MIN	MLB	35	9	9	0	26	26	150	157	24	3.1	7.5	125	43.0%	.300
2021 DC	MIN	MLB	35	4	4	0	14	14	70	73	11	3.1	7.5	58	43.0%	.300

Comparables: Clay Buchholz, Ian Kennedy, Johnny Cueto

As much as anything, baseball in 2020 was an exercise in creative human resourcing. Thus, you could pay someone like Bailey $7 million to join your rotation, start him in the home opener, stick him onto the injured list for six weeks, recall him to make a critical start down the stretch and DFA him a few days later without really alienating anyone. Back in 2019, Bailey became the latest starter to enjoy newfound success after spamming his best offspeed pitch—a vanishing splitter—while curtailing his fastball usage. After such an abbreviated season, there's a chance he gets lost in the free-agent shuffle, but Bailey ought to retain the promising sheen he had 12 months ago.

YEAR	TEAM	LVL	AGE	WHIP	ERA	DRA-	WARP	MPH	FB%	WHF	CSP
2018	LOU	AAA	32	1.35	4.78	95	0.3				
2018	CIN	MLB	32	1.64	6.09	134	-0.9	95.3	56.0%	19.5%	
2019	KC	MLB	33	1.41	4.80	111	0.3	95.1	49.3%	23.5%	
2019	OAK	MLB	33	1.20	4.30	75	1.6	95.1	52.5%	24.8%	
2020	MIN	MLB	34	1.12	3.38	110	0.0	94.2	47.4%	23.4%	
2021 FS	MIN	MLB	35	1.40	4.69	109	0.6	95.1	51.8%	23.0%	48.5%
2021 DC	MIN	MLB	35	1.40	4.69	109	0.3	95.1	51.8%	23.0%	48.5%

Minnesota Twins 2021

Jordan Balazovic   RHP
Born: 09/17/98   Age: 22   Bats: R   Throws: R
Height: 6'5"   Weight: 215   Origin: Round 5, 2016 Draft (#153 overall)

YEAR	TEAM	LVL	AGE	W	L	SV	G	GS	IP	H	HR	BB/9	K/9	K	GB%	BABIP
2018	CR	LO-A	19	7	3	0	12	11	61^2	54	5	2.6	11.4	78	46.5%	.327
2019	CR	LO-A	20	2	1	0	4	4	20^2	15	1	1.7	14.4	33	42.2%	.318
2019	FTM	HI-A	20	6	4	0	15	14	73	52	3	2.6	11.8	96	44.3%	.283
2021 FS	MIN	MLB	22	2	2	0	57	0	50	46	7	3.8	9.4	52	38.2%	.291

Comparables: Stephen Gonsalves, Lucas Giolito, Dustin May

Balazovic has never carried a starter's workload and he just lost a year to build arm strength. On paper, he has most of the ingredients we like in a back-end starter; but, between the lack of reps and a somewhat violent delivery, a future in the bullpen looks more likely than it did 12 months ago.

YEAR	TEAM	LVL	AGE	WHIP	ERA	DRA-	WARP	MPH	FB%	WHF	CSP
2018	CR	LO-A	19	1.17	3.94	65	1.6				
2019	CR	LO-A	20	0.92	2.18	40	0.8				
2019	FTM	HI-A	20	1.00	2.84	66	1.6				
2021 FS	MIN	MLB	22	1.34	4.34	103	0.2				

Dakota Chalmers   RHP
Born: 10/08/96   Age: 24   Bats: R   Throws: R
Height: 6'3"   Weight: 175   Origin: Round 3, 2015 Draft (#97 overall)

YEAR	TEAM	LVL	AGE	W	L	SV	G	GS	IP	H	HR	BB/9	K/9	K	GB%	BABIP
2019	TWI	ROK	22	1	0	0	4	4	13^1	8	0	5.4	12.8	19	64.0%	.320
2019	FTM	HI-A	22	1	1	0	5	5	21^1	12	0	6.3	12.2	29	54.5%	.273
2021 FS	MIN	MLB	24	2	3	0	57	0	50	44	7	9.1	10.8	60	41.4%	.295
2021 DC	MIN	MLB	24	1	1	0	33	0	11.3	10	1	9.1	10.8	13	41.4%	.295

Comparables: Albert Abreu, Nick Neidert, Demarcus Evans

Chalmers has three plus pitches and zero clue where any of them are going. The modern game's tolerance for "throw hard first, beg for forgiveness later" hurlers helped him land a spot on Minnesota's 40-man roster last season; perhaps he'll throw more strikes after the inevitable shift to the bullpen.

YEAR	TEAM	LVL	AGE	WHIP	ERA	DRA-	WARP	MPH	FB%	WHF	CSP
2019	TWI	ROK	22	1.20	4.05						
2019	FTM	HI-A	22	1.27	3.38	71	0.4				
2021 FS	MIN	MLB	24	1.89	6.47	132	-0.6				
2021 DC	MIN	MLB	24	1.89	6.47	132	-0.1				

Jhoan Duran   RHP

Born: 01/08/98   Age: 23   Bats: R   Throws: R
Height: 6'5"   Weight: 230   Origin: International Free Agent, 2014

YEAR	TEAM	LVL	AGE	W	L	SV	G	GS	IP	H	HR	BB/9	K/9	K	GB%	BABIP
2018	CR	LO-A	20	2	1	0	6	6	36	19	2	2.5	11.0	44	66.2%	.218
2018	KC	LO-A	20	5	4	0	15	15	64.2	69	6	3.9	9.9	71	51.1%	.348
2019	FTM	HI-A	21	2	9	0	16	15	78	63	5	3.6	11.0	95	51.6%	.317
2019	PNS	AA	21	3	3	0	7	7	37	34	2	2.2	10.0	41	63.0%	.330
2021 FS	MIN	MLB	23	9	9	0	26	26	150	138	22	4.2	8.7	145	51.6%	.283
2021 DC	MIN	MLB	23	1	1	0	8	3	13.7	12	2	4.2	8.7	13	51.6%	.283

Comparables: Adonis Medina, Johan Oviedo, Huascar Ynoa

   Duran was a consensus top-100 prospect entering 2020, an ascending arm blessed with 100-mph heat and two secondaries that should miss bats. After holding his own in Double-A the previous year, it was a bit surprising that the 23-year-old never got out of the alternate training site in '20, particularly given the trouble Minnesota had finding a stable fifth starter. Assuming nothing is amiss, he should be tracking for whatever constitutes a high-minors assignment this spring, and could debut as soon as this summer.

YEAR	TEAM	LVL	AGE	WHIP	ERA	DRA-	WARP	MPH	FB%	WHF	CSP
2018	CR	LO-A	20	0.81	2.00	55	1.1				
2018	KC	LO-A	20	1.50	4.73	75	1.3				
2019	FTM	HI-A	21	1.21	3.23	90	0.6				
2019	PNS	AA	21	1.16	4.86	128	-0.6				
2021 FS	MIN	MLB	23	1.39	4.52	106	0.9				
2021 DC	MIN	MLB	23	1.39	4.52	106	0.1				

Ian Hamilton RHP

Born: 06/16/95 Age: 26 Bats: R Throws: R
Height: 6'1" Weight: 200 Origin: Round 11, 2016 Draft (#326 overall)

YEAR	TEAM	LVL	AGE	W	L	SV	G	GS	IP	H	HR	BB/9	K/9	K	GB%	BABIP
2018	BIR	AA	23	2	1	12	21	0	25¹	20	0	4.3	12.1	34	45.2%	.328
2018	CHA	AAA	23	1	1	10	22	0	26¹	18	2	1.4	9.6	28	46.2%	.262
2018	CHW	MLB	23	1	2	0	10	0	8	6	2	2.2	5.6	5	48.0%	.174
2019	CHA	AAA	24	0	2	3	16	0	16¹	28	4	1.7	11.0	20	50.9%	.480
2020	CHW	MLB	25	0	0	0	4	0	4	4	0	11.2	9.0	4	27.3%	.364
2021 FS	MIN	MLB	26	2	2	0	57	0	50	44	6	4.0	9.1	50	43.9%	.286
2021 DC	MIN	MLB	26	1	1	0	29	0	11.3	10	1	4.0	9.1	11	43.9%	.286

Comparables: Edubray Ramos, Jake Newberry, Thyago Vieira

As far as Hamiltons go, Ian's luck with flying objects at his face is at least a grade better than others. But while he's re-emerged from a spring training car accident and a foul ball that struck him in the dugout, breaking his jaw and ending his 2019 season, the high-90s velocity he once touted to paper over other irregularities has not. At 93-95 mph, a lot of Hamilton's quirks—a crossfire throwing motion with a unique arm action, his slider a bizarre product of an old attempt to teach himself a changeup and acts accordingly strange—turned into warts, and he found himself bouncing along the waiver wire, from the White Sox to the Mariners and then to the Phillies. Hamilton is a plus athlete, whose washboard abs still stack well against any other reliever, and those sorts of guys often figure it out with time, patience and recovery. But something will need to change in his recent trendline for Hamilton to appear in the next version of this book.

YEAR	TEAM	LVL	AGE	WHIP	ERA	DRA-	WARP	MPH	FB%	WHF	CSP
2018	BIR	AA	23	1.26	1.78	73	0.4				
2018	CHA	AAA	23	0.84	1.71	74	0.4				
2018	CHW	MLB	23	1.00	4.50	75	0.1	98.1	70.1%	23.7%	
2019	CHA	AAA	24	1.90	9.92	134	0.0				
2020	CHW	MLB	25	2.25	4.50	107	0.0	95.8	74.7%	36.4%	
2021 FS	MIN	MLB	26	1.34	3.95	92	0.5	96.5	73.2%	32.3%	45.6%
2021 DC	MIN	MLB	26	1.34	3.95	92	0.1	96.5	73.2%	32.3%	45.6%

Jefry Rodriguez RHP

Born: 07/26/93 Age: 27 Bats: R Throws: R
Height: 6'6" Weight: 232 Origin: International Free Agent, 2012

YEAR	TEAM	LVL	AGE	W	L	SV	G	GS	IP	H	HR	BB/9	K/9	K	GB%	BABIP
2018	HBG	AA	24	5	3	0	13	13	68	55	6	3.7	9.5	72	51.9%	.282
2018	SYR	AAA	24	2	2	0	6	6	32^2	32	0	4.1	8.3	30	44.8%	.340
2018	WAS	MLB	24	3	3	0	14	8	52	43	8	6.4	6.8	39	42.9%	.245
2019	COL	AAA	25	1	0	0	5	3	21^2	16	1	4.6	6.6	16	52.5%	.250
2019	CLE	MLB	25	1	5	0	10	8	46^2	48	5	4.0	6.4	33	48.3%	.301
2021 FS	MIN	MLB	27	2	3	0	57	0	50	48	7	5.1	8.0	44	46.5%	.289

Comparables: Scott Barlow, Spencer Turnbull, Keury Mella

Last season was a case of déjà vu for Rodríguez, as well as a case of ne l'a pas vu for everyone else. He was *hors de combat* for the Opening Day roster with a back injury before the same shoulder trouble that interrupted his '19 campaign provided the *dénouement* of a frustrating season. May his third season prove to be le charme.

YEAR	TEAM	LVL	AGE	WHIP	ERA	DRA-	WARP	MPH	FB%	WHF	CSP
2018	HBG	AA	24	1.22	3.31	71	1.6				
2018	SYR	AAA	24	1.44	3.58	95	0.3				
2018	WAS	MLB	24	1.54	5.71	164	-1.3	97.5	65.0%	21.0%	
2019	COL	AAA	25	1.25	4.15	86	0.5				
2019	CLE	MLB	25	1.48	4.63	143	-0.6	96.3	70.0%	18.8%	
2021 FS	MIN	MLB	27	1.53	4.87	109	0.0	96.8	68.1%	19.6%	46.6%

Taylor Rogers LHP

Born: 12/17/90   Age: 30   Bats: L   Throws: L
Height: 6'3"   Weight: 190   Origin: Round 11, 2012 Draft (#340 overall)

YEAR	TEAM	LVL	AGE	W	L	SV	G	GS	IP	H	HR	BB/9	K/9	K	GB%	BABIP
2018	MIN	MLB	27	1	2	2	72	0	68¹	49	3	2.1	9.9	75	43.7%	.282
2019	MIN	MLB	28	2	4	30	60	0	69	58	8	1.4	11.7	90	49.7%	.312
2020	MIN	MLB	29	2	4	9	21	0	20	26	2	1.8	10.8	24	43.5%	.400
2021 FS	MIN	MLB	30	2	2	16	57	0	50	45	5	2.2	10.0	55	46.4%	.303
2021 DC	MIN	MLB	30	2	2	16	55	0	56.7	51	6	2.2	10.0	63	46.4%	.303

Comparables: Dylan Floro, Andrew Chafin, Tyler Duffey

As a general principle, you shouldn't place too much emphasis on 2020 numbers, for obvious reasons. With Rogers though, there are some underlying indicators that suggest he's taken a step backward. First, his velocity dropped. His average fastball velocity didn't dip much, but he lost more than a tick and a half off his slider from 2019, and not surprisingly batters fared much better against it in 2020. He's also now a two-pitch pitcher. The curve had long been one of his best offerings, but he's felt less comfortable throwing it in recent seasons and all but shelved it last year. More predictability and lower velocity is a bad combination, and if it's the new normal, Minnesota probably shouldn't count on him as their relief ace anymore.

YEAR	TEAM	LVL	AGE	WHIP	ERA	DRA-	WARP	MPH	FB%	WHF	CSP
2018	MIN	MLB	27	0.95	2.63	74	1.3	95.2	53.0%	27.1%	
2019	MIN	MLB	28	1.00	2.61	57	1.9	96.2	50.1%	26.2%	
2020	MIN	MLB	29	1.50	4.05	81	0.4	95.8	54.5%	23.6%	
2021 FS	MIN	MLB	30	1.16	3.29	81	0.8	95.9	51.9%	25.7%	53.7%
2021 DC	MIN	MLB	30	1.16	3.29	81	0.9	95.9	51.9%	25.7%	53.7%

Devin Smeltzer LHP

Born: 09/07/95   Age: 25   Bats: R   Throws: L
Height: 6'3"   Weight: 195   Origin: Round 5, 2016 Draft (#161 overall)

YEAR	TEAM	LVL	AGE	W	L	SV	G	GS	IP	H	HR	BB/9	K/9	K	GB%	BABIP
2018	TUL	AA	22	5	5	0	23	14	83^2	94	9	2.0	7.2	67	37.2%	.323
2018	CHA	AA	22	0	0	4	10	0	12	14	0	1.5	12.0	16	30.6%	.400
2019	PNS	AA	23	3	1	0	5	5	30	19	0	0.9	9.9	33	42.3%	.268
2019	ROC	AAA	23	1	4	0	15	14	74^1	68	14	2.3	8.6	71	37.6%	.274
2019	MIN	MLB	23	2	2	1	11	6	49	50	8	2.2	7.0	38	37.7%	.294
2020	MIN	MLB	24	2	0	0	7	1	16	19	2	2.8	8.4	15	35.3%	.354
2021 FS	MIN	MLB	25	9	9	0	26	26	150	150	26	2.7	8.3	138	37.7%	.292
2021 DC	MIN	MLB	25	5	4	0	22	8	74.3	74	12	2.7	8.3	69	37.7%	.292

Comparables: Ranger Suárez, Nestor Cortes, Lewis Thorpe

Aesthetically, Smeltzer brings the funk. He starts his delivery by gyrating toward second base and then sharply merry-go-rounding his way to the plate, which has the effect of a man trying to dislocate his pitching shoulder and stab his catcher at the same time. Everything's a bit less interesting once the ball leaves his hand. The southpaw lacks a plus secondary to buttress mediocre velocity and if he's to have a long career, he'll need to survive on guile and deception.

YEAR	TEAM	LVL	AGE	WHIP	ERA	DRA-	WARP	MPH	FB%	WHF	CSP
2018	TUL	AA	22	1.35	4.73	85	1.0				
2018	CHA	AA	22	1.33	3.00	63	0.3				
2019	PNS	AA	23	0.73	0.60	54	0.8				
2019	ROC	AAA	23	1.17	3.63	80	2.0				
2019	MIN	MLB	23	1.27	3.86	114	0.0	90.8	45.8%	20.7%	
2020	MIN	MLB	24	1.50	6.75	118	0.0	89.1	33.2%	25.0%	
2021 FS	MIN	MLB	25	1.30	4.41	104	1.1	90.2	41.3%	22.2%	48.9%
2021 DC	MIN	MLB	25	1.30	4.41	104	0.3	90.2	41.3%	22.2%	48.9%

Lewis Thorpe LHP

Born: 11/23/95 Age: 25 Bats: R Throws: L
Height: 6'1" Weight: 218 Origin: International Free Agent, 2012

YEAR	TEAM	LVL	AGE	W	L	SV	G	GS	IP	H	HR	BB/9	K/9	K	GB%	BABIP
2018	CHA	AA	22	8	4	0	22	21	108	105	13	2.5	10.9	131	37.1%	.329
2018	ROC	AAA	22	0	3	0	4	4	21²	20	3	2.5	10.8	26	42.9%	.321
2019	ROC	AAA	23	5	4	0	20	19	96¹	91	13	2.3	11.1	119	39.9%	.322
2019	MIN	MLB	23	3	2	0	12	2	27²	38	3	3.3	10.1	31	34.9%	.438
2020	MIN	MLB	24	0	1	0	7	1	16¹	24	4	5.5	5.5	10	35.1%	.377
2021 FS	MIN	MLB	25	9	8	0	26	26	150	143	22	3.7	8.9	148	37.6%	.292
2021 DC	MIN	MLB	25	6	4	0	46	6	70	67	10	3.7	8.9	69	37.6%	.292

Comparables: Justus Sheffield, Cionel Pérez, Ranger Suárez

In 2019, Thorpe was a feel-good story, a perennially injured prospect who finally put his arm troubles behind him and made his big-league debut. In 2020? Well, at least there weren't any fans around to see it.

YEAR	TEAM	LVL	AGE	WHIP	ERA	DRA-	WARP	MPH	FB%	WHF	CSP
2018	CHA	AA	22	1.25	3.58	82	1.8				
2018	ROC	AAA	22	1.20	3.32	78	0.4				
2019	ROC	AAA	23	1.20	4.58	72	2.9				
2019	MIN	MLB	23	1.73	6.18	109	0.0	93.3	50.0%	27.9%	
2020	MIN	MLB	24	2.08	6.06	180	-0.6	92.3	47.4%	20.7%	
2021 FS	MIN	MLB	25	1.37	4.34	101	1.3	92.9	48.8%	24.6%	49.6%
2021 DC	MIN	MLB	25	1.37	4.34	101	0.4	92.9	48.8%	24.6%	49.6%

Twins Prospects

The State of the System:
The Twins' system remains deep enough that I am once again annoyed by some of the names I couldn't make room for in the top ten.

The Top Ten:

─────── ★ ★ ★ *2021 Top 101 Prospect* **#31** ★ ★ ★ ───────

1 **Royce Lewis** SS OFP: 70 ETA: Late-2021 or early-2022
Born: 06/05/99 Age: 22 Bats: R Throws: R Height: 6'2" Weight: 200
Origin: Round 1, 2017 Draft (#1 overall)

The Report: We've written as extensively on Lewis as any other prospect over the past few years. We'll start with the good stuff: Lewis has lightning-quick hands and generates a whole lot of bat speed with them. At times, with his best swings, we've projected him as a plus hitter. He projects for above-average-to-plus power. He has the defensive chops to play nearly anywhere on the diamond—short, second, third, center, you name it. And he runs very well too. There's true five-tool potential here.

There's also a level of hit tool variance which is nearly unprecedented for a former No. 1 overall pick who has already reached Double-A and is still a great prospect. Lewis gets seriously out of sync between his upper and lower halves, with a ton of moving parts, and his swing is inconsistent at best and kind of a disaster at worst.

Development Track: There's obviously an outcome where everything comes together in a flash for Lewis and he's a star with an average-or-better hit tool—we have people on staff who believe in that outcome—but our confidence in that solution is no higher than last year, and time is not an ally here. Lewis wasn't called up from the alternate site, which you can read a few ways. He didn't have to be added to the 40-man this offseason, so there were reasons within the context of roster construction not to call him up. But at the same time, if he *had*
gotten everything together, he probably would've pushed his way to the MLB roster, right? Jeffers did, and Kirilloff did, even if just for the playoffs. In the 2020 video we saw, the swing issues Lewis has been battling for the past couple years didn't exactly look like they'd gone away.

Variance: Extreme. Somehow it got higher here?

J.P. Breen's Fantasy Take: Lewis is a tough dynasty prospect to value. On one hand, he has five-category upside, if it all comes together. He's easily a top-two-round talent in that case. On the other hand, if the swing issues don't improve, we're talking about a low-average super utility player who would derive most of his fantasy value from stolen bases and volume—though volume would be tough to come by if he's hitting .230 with a sub-.300 OBP. Here's the main dynasty problem: Lewis's value (currently our 15th-ranked dynasty prospect) reflects his upside, not the likelihood that he ever reaches that upside. He's basically impossible to acquire, and it'd be foolish to pay the going rate, given his extreme volatility. If you're already rostering him, you'll probably have to hold him. If you don't have him, you won't like the asking price.

★ ★ ★ *2021 Top 101 Prospect* **#71** ★ ★ ★

2

Alex Kirilloff RF   OFP: 60   ETA: Debuted in 2020
Born: 11/09/97   Age: 23   Bats: L   Throws: L   Height: 6'2"   Weight: 195
Origin: Round 1, 2016 Draft (#15 overall)

The Report: For a system that we are quite bullish on overall, we've been skeptical about the top two names here in recent years. The Q+D on Kirilloff: A post-draft breakout in short-season coming off a cold weather prep career made us all think perhaps there was more in the tank. Tommy John surgery cost him the next season, so we had to wait to see it at full-season ball. His performance on the field in 2018 was quite good, but the underlying swing had us skeptical about just how loud the hit and power tools would be given the corner profile. In 2019 Kirilloff dealt with a wrist injury and played almost as much first base as outfield. There's the potential for a plus-or-better hit tool with plus power, but he can get pull-power-happy and out of sync, leading to suboptimal contact. And he doesn't consistently lift the ball either, struggling to hit for corner bat game power above Low-A. Yes, there's that pesky wrist injury mention again, but it's all a bit muddled still.

Development Track: Kirilloff was a surprise add to the playoff roster for an injured Josh Donaldson after spending the summer at the alternate site. Conversely to the Royce Lewis discussion above, you could read into it that the Twins thought Kirilloff was the best option for that spot even though it wasn't a straight like-for-like swap. We're not going to fill the evaluation vacuum by reading too much into his four Wild Card Series plate appearances, but it did appear like he was still stuck between his 2018 and 2019 swings. Kirilloff could use some consolidation time in Triple-A, but once you are willing to start a player in the playoffs—and opened a theoretical spot for him by non-tendering Eddie Rosario—well, one could look at these as signals.

Variance: High. We don't think Kirilloff will have the weird orphan "Postseason Batting" baseball-reference page for long, the range of outcomes can go to fringe regular if the bat merely plays a little above average, to frequent All-Star if he unlocks (re-unlocks) something in the swing.

J.P. Breen's Fantasy Take: Assuming he winds up at first base, Kirilloff has an Eric Hosmer feel about him. That is, the average is good and the raw power is present, but there's a significant risk that none of those skills transition over to in-game power—making him a 20-homer, solid-average first baseman who has the occasional hot stretch. Kirilloff is more interesting as a corner outfielder, just not as much as you might think. Perhaps he puts everything together in 2021. I just don't plan on being the one who's betting on that outcome.

────── ★ ★ ★ *2021 Top 101 Prospect* **#83** ★ ★ ★ ──────

3 **Trevor Larnach** **RF** OFP: 60 ETA: 2021, as needed
Born: 02/26/97 Age: 24 Bats: L Throws: R Height: 6'4" Weight: 223
Origin: Round 1, 2018 Draft (#20 overall)

The Report: Larnach and Kirilloff were merely one spot apart on the Top 101 coming into 2020. They remain close to a pick 'em of corner bats with plus hit and power potential who haven't dominated the minor leagues to the point where we are supremely confident they'd be plus regulars in the majors. Larnach's swing is more geared for power than Kirilloff, but his slugging percentages have mostly started with a four. The soon-to-be 24-year-old had a sturdy, mature frame, so any further power gains will have to come from lifting some of those doubles in the gap over the fence. Larnach is a perfectly adequate corner outfielder, but that still leaves a world of value in the gap between being a .270, 20 home-run hitter in the majors, versus .290 and 30.

Development Track: Flipping Kirilloff and Larnach this year isn't merely because the Twins chose to add one to the playoff roster over the other—Kirilloff was going to need to be added to the 40 anyway, Larnach wasn't—but it does point us in a direction. That said, the gap between the two remains fairly insignificant with Kirilloff having more upside. That's what wins out this year. The alternate site was roughly an appropriate level of competition for where Larnach was as a prospect, and he should be ready for the majors sometime in 2021.

Variance: High. While the top-line Double-A numbers were a tad better than Kirilloff's—however much you want to read into a month of performance—The K-rate did spike some, and Larnach's swing is geared for more swing-and-miss along with the additional game pop.

J.P. Breen's Fantasy Take: The Twins' minor-league system reminds me of *Game of Thrones*. Many of your intelligent friends hype it up, but when you sit down and finally dig into the beginning of it, you realize that you're looking at something solid enough that has the potential to be incredible. Larnach is the third consecutive Twins dynasty prospect who is profile-over-production, whose value treats him like a safe 30-homer corner masher, when he only hit 13 bombs in 542 PA between High-A and Double-A as a 22-year-old. Let's hope Larnach reaches his potential more fully than George R. R. Martin's series did.

4 Ryan Jeffers C   OFP: 60   ETA: Debuted in 2020
Born: 06/03/97   Age: 24   Bats: R   Throws: R   Height: 6'4"   Weight: 235
Origin: Round 2, 2018 Draft (#59 overall)

The Report: We noted Jeffers was moving fast last year when he made it to Double-A in his first full pro season. He's not the world's most exhilarating prospect in written form—average hit tool projection, above-average power—but he's turned out to be much more advanced than we thought. More importantly, he's turned out to be a pretty nifty framer and overall defender despite his size. A bunch of 5s and 55s plays better behind the plate than anywhere else, at least in the age where there's like all of five good two-way catchers in all of MLB at any given time.

Development Track: Jeffers was unexpectedly called up in 2020 just two years after being drafted. That's very fast for a catcher, and he was an above-average framer in the small sample. His hitting stats weren't facially hugely impressive, but he hit the ball

hard

: 91.6 mph average exit velocity, with six batted balls out of 38 over 105 mph and a max of 112.9 mph. His stock is rising.

Variance: Medium, although that's low as catchers go. There's only a couple catching prospects more likely to be a decent regular or semi-regular.

J.P. Breen's Fantasy Take: Jeffers has hit .270-plus at every professional stop, save his 2019 stint in High-A, but the Florida State League is rarely friendly to hitters. Jeffers could be a top-10 fantasy catcher. Only seven catchers hit .270-plus with at least 15 homers in 2019. Jeffers has the skills and track record to join that club as quickly as 2021. The presence of Mitch Garver on the roster, however, makes forecasting when he'll get the chance to log 350 PA very difficult.

5 Jhoan Duran RHP   OFP: 60   ETA: 2021, as needed
Born: 01/08/98   Age: 23   Bats: R   Throws: R   Height: 6'5"   Weight: 230
Origin: International Free Agent, 2014

The Report: If you were building a starting pitching prospect on paper you could do far worse than Duran. He's a 6-foot-5, well-built righty. He's tossed more than 100 innings in each of his last two actual seasons. Oh yeah, he has three potential plus pitches, including a fastball that routinely hits triple digits, a high-80s power curve, and a sinker/split hybrid. The minor league performance has matched the stuff, as he has posted 25%+ K-rates in 2018 and 2019. He generally finds the zone with his plus stuff. This sounds like one of the better pitching prospects in baseball, no? But if I may put on my bucket hat and Kohl's clearance rack color block polo for a moment, the games aren't played on paper, sport-o. Duran's delivery is high effort and the command profile has lagged behind the control. The splittish thing is a neat pitch, but it's not a true armside option against lefties, who had some success against him in 2019. So there remains some reliever risk. We're mostly nitpicking, but nitpickability is the difference between a Top 50 prospect in baseball and merely in consideration for the back of the 101.

Development Track: It's entirely possible Duran could have helped the 2020 Twins pitching staff on merit. And I'm a little surprised they didn't try to use him as a 'pen weapon late in the season and into the postseason, but honestly their pitching staff ran deep enough if it would have been a bit of a luxury. And you'd want to keep him stretched out as a starter for 2021 where he could make the most near-term impact. I'd expect Duran to start in Triple-A, but he could easily be the first arm up, and it's not impossible he beats out Randy Dobnak and Devin Smeltzer with a strong camp if the Twins don't bolster their rotation elsewhere.

Variance: Medium. If Duran does end up in the 'pen long term, the fastball/curve combo will play in high leverage. There's the usual pitcher health risks too of course.

J.P. Breen's Fantasy Take: Duran has a lot going for him. He has the stuff and the track record to make one comfortable that he'll miss bats in the majors; he has the size you'd ideally want in a starter; and he's poised to make his big-league debut in 2021. However, the questions about his command and his potential platoon split make Duran a potential roto risk in terms of rates. Overall, you're looking at a borderline top-100 dynasty prospect.

6. Jordan Balazovic   RHP   OFP: 55   ETA: 2021 or 2022
Born: 09/17/98   Age: 22   Bats: R   Throws: R   Height: 6'5"   Weight: 215
Origin: Round 5, 2016 Draft (#153 overall)

The Report: When drafting projectable—albeit ultra skinny—cold-weather pitchers, you hope to see them blossom into what Balazovic is turning into. A slow mover to date, the 6-foot-5 righty has continued to add strength and could be in line for a big league promotion in the coming year. His extremely long levers act as a slight-of-hand during his delivery, with his mid-90s heater getting on hitters quickly. The release point is lower than you'd think for such a tall pitcher, which gives the fastball a sideways sink in its action. Despite the late movement, it doesn't play like a typical sinker because of all the deception. Atypical describes a lot of his game, being able to repeat his mechanics and throw a lot of strikes for his age while also mixing in at least two average-to-better breaking balls is a credit to his body control.

Development Track: The knock until now was the concern over whether his frame could add the necessary weight to survive a full season of starting. There have been no hiccups yet, succeeding at every challenge thrown his way thus far.

Now as he begins to round out his game in preparation for The Show, what's left is continued work on a changeup that should be able to play off his fastball shape against lefty batters.

Variance: Medium. Nothing about what he does on the mound is conventional by almost any measure. He shouldn't have such control of his pitches, his arm should have had something barking by now, and yet he's proving what works for him is still getting better.

J.P. Breen's Fantasy Take: Balazovic profiles as a safe (at least, safe for a pitching prospect) bet to make it as a starter. When we normally hear about deceptive fastballs, they're struggling to stay above 90 mph, but the right-hander runs it into the mid-90s and misses bats with it. Balazovic also throws strikes and has a pair of breaking balls. I love high-floor profiles when they're paired with moderate upside, and it's not a stretch to think that, if the changeup develops a bit, Balazovic can flirt with an SP2 season or two. I'd take Balazovic over Duran in both redraft and dynasty formats in 2021.

7 Matt Canterino   RHP   OFP: 55   ETA: 2022
Born: 12/14/97   Age: 23   Bats: R   Throws: R   Height: 6'2"   Weight: 222
Origin: Round 2, 2019 Draft (#54 overall)

The Report: The Twins used their second-round pick in 2019 on a very second-roundish college arm. Canterino was a three-year starter at Rice who missed bats with a potential plus fastball/slider combo. The minimal physical projection, along with a hitchy delivery made it easy to cast him as a 95-and-a-slider type reliever. Which we did last year. He had upside past that, but was an OFP 50 type with relief risk in a very good and deep system, so it would be easy for him to get lost in the shuffle and end up, say, 18th on last year's Twins list.

Development Track: One of the themes of the prospect team's Fungo essay in this year's Baseball Prospectus *Annual* is the difficulty in identifying breakout prospects given the dearth of data for players who didn't accrue major league time. With Canterino though there were two notable skill changes: He added a tick or two on the fastball, but more importantly, his changeup—previously a below-average afterthought in his arsenal, now has plus projection. That rounds out a starter's arsenal with three potential above-average MLB offerings. We need to see how it all works in real games, and the delivery and command concerns remain, but the arrow is clearly pointing up.

Variance: High. The gains in the profile haven't been seen in games yet, and he might give the velocity back on a more regular pitching schedule. Also worth noting that while Rice isn't as Ricey as they once were, Canterino was used heavily there by modern college pitching standards. There's positive variance here as well though. If we see the improvements translate on-field in 2021 he's not all that far off from a Top-101 arm.

J.P. Breen's Fantasy Take: File Canterino's name away and take him as a late-round pick in your dynasty supplemental draft. I'm reluctant to get too high on the righty until we see him throwing (and producing) every fifth day in Double-A this season. However, he's worth a speculative add in deeper dynasties, as he'll miss enough bats to be rosterable in all formats, if the latest reports prove accurate. And dynasty owners rarely have time to wait and see whether a prospect breakout is legit. Pounce early and cross your fingers.

8   Aaron Sabato   1B   OFP: 50   ETA: 2023
Born: 06/04/99   Age: 22   Bats: R   Throws: R   Height: 6'2"   Weight: 230
Origin: Round 1, 2020 Draft (#27 overall)

The Report: Picture in your mind the prototypical slugging first baseman. What does he look like? A largely built, sometimes wide-bodied, plodding strongman who hits the ball really far and needs a position on the field to hide his lack of foot-speed and lateral movement. That appropriately describes Sabato, the first-round pick whose value will likely be exclusive to how much he hits. It's more power than contact—he's still able to work a count and take his fair share of walks—and the swing is catered to generate loft thanks to his back posture bent slightly at the waist. The above-average bat-speed also helps with the exit velo, staying mostly in control without selling out too much for hard contact.

Development Track: While technically "old" for a draft-eligible sophomore, he's around the same age as most juniors in this class. The calling card being the power bat, he will need to see as much quality pitching as possible to be tested. His body is ready-made as is, the defense and running will likely plateau soon if not already. Get the man in the lineup and see where it takes him.

Variance: High. If it turns out his swing can be exposed and he can't adjust, there is little left he can contribute.

J.P. Breen's Fantasy Take: A top-20 dynasty player in the 2020 draft class, Sabato must hit for both average and power to be both fantasy and real-life relevant. Currently, as the above report indicates, it's power-over-hit, which is readily obtainable from a first baseman. He'll get popped earlier than he probably should be in offseason supplemental drafts, as first-round first basemen often are, but he has a legit pathway to being an impact big-league bat.

9   Keoni Cavaco   SS   OFP: 50   ETA: 2025
Born: 06/02/01   Age: 20   Bats: R   Throws: R   Height: 6'2"   Weight: 195
Origin: Round 1, 2019 Draft (#13 overall)

The Report: No player in the 2019 draft had as much helium attached to their name as Cavaco, whose growth spurt and sterling spring high school season helped him fly up draft boards, ultimately landing with the Twins 13th pick in the first round. The 6-foot-2 19-year-old is strong, and has smooth transitions with his hands that could play at multiple positions, and with measurables off the charts. Despite the present strength, he still projects for more, and the raw power is present even when the swing gets a little disconnected. He's the kind of player you dream on after a lot of little things go right, and he needs more experience to get there.

Development Track: Add him to the group of players who were likely most impacted by not having a year's worth of games to help them developmentally. He was hampered by a minor injury after being drafted and was expected to get his feet underneath him with a full 2020 campaign. Slotted in at shortstop during his brief pro debut, it will be interesting to see how much rust is attached to the glove in 2021. He has the ability to cover any number of positions, including second, third, or perhaps even center field.

Variance: Extreme. There's nothing to suggest he couldn't become a stud, but the delta remains huge given that it remains mostly projection at this stage. Such a high variance on a young player, we look forward to getting a better look soon.

J.P. Breen's Fantasy Take: Cavaco is a high-variance, high-reward prospect. Unlike Royce Lewis, however, Cavaco isn't a consensus top-100 dynasty prospect, thanks to injuries and the COVID-19 shutdown of Minor League Baseball. That should make the gamble much more attractive to dynasty owners. Cavaco is a hyped prospect who could fly into the top-30 prospects with a big 2021 campaign. In that sense, now is the time to acquire him. Conversely, he could spin his wheels in 2021 and quickly be forgotten like Estevan Florial.

10 Brent Rooker OF   OFP: 50   ETA: Debuted in 2020
Born: 11/01/94   Age: 26   Bats: R   Throws: R   Height: 6'3"   Weight: 225
Origin: Round 1, 2017 Draft (#35 overall)

The Report: The Twins drafted Rooker twice, finally getting their man as a redshirt junior, following a season where he laid waste to the SEC to the tune of a .387/.495/.810 slash line. He's hit everywhere since. Rooker is not quite the hulking corner slugger you might envision, he's stooping but on the lean side, shorter with the bat path than you might expect, but with the requisite strength, stiffness, and leverage to bring plenty of pop but commensurate swing-and-miss as well. If he hits .250, the walks and power make him a useful regular, and he turns on enough inside fastballs you might project him to get there. Rooker also swings through enough breakers in the zone where you worry he might be a Quad-A slugger. But so far no level of pitching has been able to keep him from his appointed mashing.

Development Track: Rooker got a spot of major league time when Max Kepler hit the IL in early September and cracked his first major league home run and a couple extra base hits to go with it. He's 26 now and there's some surety in the profile. Given enough playing time he can hit you 30 home runs, get on base enough to prop up fringy batting averages, and stand in a few different spots. You're buying the bat here, and it's a good bat.

Variance: Low. Rooker has never not hit, up to and including his brief 2020 Twins cameo, but the underlying offensive tools might not be loud enough to carry the overall profile past useful. But hey, that's useful.

J.P. Breen's Fantasy Take: Rooker has strong Hunter Renfroe vibes, and not the Hunter Renfroe from the first half of 2019. The breaking-ball issues will always make Rooker a platoon risk, and the power needs to be special to overcome his projected AVG and SB shortcomings in fantasy. Treat him like a fringe top-250 dynasty prospect.

The Prospects You Meet Outside The Top Ten

Prospects to dream on a little bit

Josh Winder   RHP   Born: 10/11/96   Age: 24   Bats: R   Throws: R   Height: 6'5"   Weight: 210   Origin: Round 7, 2018 Draft (#214 overall)

The Twins' seventh round pick in 2018 out of VMI, Winder showed up at instructs this year sitting mid-90s with his fastball, a big bump over his college velocity. He has a full mix of secondaries backing the fastball, all of which have above-average potential. Like with Canterino—and really even more so given their respective track records—we'll need to see the stuff in a more normal year before we jot down these improvements in ink, but you could certainly argue on upside and perhaps even OFP that he deserves to pip Rooker for the 10th spot in the system.

Misael Urbina   CF   Born: 04/26/02   Age: 19   Bats: R   Throws: R   Height: 6'0"   Weight: 175   Origin: International Free Agent, 2018

We got strong reports on Urbina in 2019, but tend to play it safe with IFAs with minimal stateside experience. It was going to be tough for Urbina to "break out" in 2020 given he was thrown to the lions, or at least a bunch of the pitchers residing in the top half of the list. Urbina held his own at the alternate site despite the degree of difficulty, which is all you can really ask of your teenaged hitting prospects in 2020.

MLB bats, but less upside than you'd like

Gilberto Celestino   CF   Born: 02/13/99   Age: 22   Bats: R   Throws: L   Height: 6'0"   Weight: 170   Origin: International Free Agent, 2015

Celestino also had a case for No. 10 in the system, a ranking he held this time last year. He's a near mirror image of Rooker, a center fielder who can go get it in the gaps, but has limited upside with the bat. He's not an empty wizard, to quote one of my predecessors, and even average production with the stick would make him a solid or better regular. He shows good bat speed, but not much loft so he will need to sting a fair amount of doubles into the gap to make it as an everyday center fielder. For now we will bet on the player we are more confident will hit (to be the 10th best prospect in a good system).

Interesting Draft Follows

Alerick Soularie   OF   Born: 07/05/99   Age: 22   Bats: R   Throws: R   Height: 6'0"   Weight: 175   Origin: Round 2, 2020 Draft (#59 overall)
A big time producer, first in JuCo and then at the University of Tennessee, Soularie's game can best be summarized by the characteristics of his swing: It's in-between. He's not really an infielder, lacking the arm to play anywhere but second base. He's not really a center fielder, with decent speed it's not the plus wheels or instincts you'd prefer there. Not really a power hitter, despite showing an ability to carry his raw power into games thanks to an innate ability to lift the ball. The hands get really loose as the pitch approaches, finishing belt-high with an elongated stride. It's funky, but it works. Fact is: he gets the job done, it isn't always pretty, and maybe with some refinement there's more there.

Marco Raya   Born: 08/07/02   Age: 18   Bats: R   Throws: R   Height: 6'0"   Weight: 165   Origin: Round 4, 2020 Draft (#128 overall)
The Twins' fourth-round pick in 2020, Raya is a non-traditional Texas prep arm. Listed at 6-foot-0 (so probably 5-foot-10) and with minimal physical projection, he's a relatively advanced high school arm who will show four potentially average-or-better pitches. The fastball is low-90s with good spin, but you may not wring much more out there. His loose, uptempo delivery only has mild effort given his size, and he's worth ... well, a follow to see how the secondaries progress under pro instruction.

Top Talents 25 and Under (as of 4/1/2021):

1. Royce Lewis, IF/OF
2. Luis Arraez, 2B
3. Alex Kirilloff, OF/1B
4. Trevor Larnach, OF
5. Ryan Jeffers, C
6. Jhoan Duran, RHP
7. Jordan Balazovic, RHP
8. Matt Canterino, RHP
9. Aaron Sabato, 1B
10. Jorge Alcala, RHP

Luis Arraez is now a .331 hitter over 487 plate appearances in the majors, which is a lot more than you can reasonably fluke your way into. He's probably not *that* good because hardly anybody is a true talent .330-plus hitter, but Arraez clearly has elite bat-to-ball skills. There's little power here and really the hit tool is carrying the entire profile, but all that's okay if you're a batting champion-in-waiting, and he might be.

Just tagging along on the bottom of the list is reliever Jorge Alcala. Alcala was the last player omitted from our top 20 prospects last year, when he was still mid-relief conversion. He made the full-time switch for 2020, and his velocity jumped more consistently into the upper-90s; he also threw nearly as many hard sliders as he threw fastballs, along with the occasional hard change. He was very effective, and seems headed down a late-game reliever path.

Part 3: Featured Articles

Twins All-Time Top 10 Players

by Rob Mains

POSITION PLAYERS

JOE MAUER, C/1B (2004-2018)
Concussions robbed us of the opportunity to see where the St. Paul native and no. 1 pick in the 2001 draft would've ranked all-time among catchers. His career .306/.388/.439 final line is a disappointment only in relation to his .334/.416/.491 peak from 2006 to 2010 when he won three batting titles and was a three-time Gold Glove catcher.

JOE JUDGE, 1B (1915-1932)
His 2,084 games played trails only Killebrew and Rice in franchise history. Like Rice, his home run totals didn't tick up when the lively ball ended the Deadball Era, but he was a high on-base hitter (.379 OBP as a Senator) with a .299 batting average who was good on the basepaths. He was considered an outstanding first baseman despite standing only 5'8".

HARMON KILLEBREW, 1B/3B/LF (1954-1974)
It's been nearly a half century since Killer called Metropolitan Stadium home, but his 14 at-bats per homer as a Twin still ranks fifth all-time behind Mark McGwire, Babe Ruth, Barry Bonds, and Jim Thome among players with at least 5,000 plate appearances. Only Ruth hit 40 or more homers in a season more frequently than Killebrew's eight. And he struck out only 8 percent more frequently than he walked, resulting in a .378 OBP to go with his .514 slugging percentage.

BUDDY MYER, 2B (1925-27, 1929-1941)
He moved from shortstop to third base, from Washington to Boston and back again, hitting up and down the lineup, all with below-average offensive performance until he became the Senators' full-time leadoff hitter and second

baseman in August 1930. He was the sparkplug for the last good Senators team, batting .303 with a .393 on base percentage for Washington. He was at the center of a huge brawl between the Senators and Yankees in 1933 that's viewed as one of the catalysts for the team's pennant that year.

ROD CAREW, 2B/1B (1967-1978)
Fifteen straight years batting over .300. Six batting titles, including four straight seasons. Named to the All-Star team every year in Minnesota. Rookie of the Year in 1967, MVP a decade later. And he wasn't just a singles hitter: He had a .393 on-base percentage and a .448 slugging percentage in Minnesota. A devastating hitter of a kind presently absent from the game.

CLYDE MILAN, OF (1907-1922)
Milan (MILL-in) isn't well-remembered now but he was one of the top leadoff hitters of his era. He had a career .353 on base percentage and stole a franchise-record 495 bases. His 88 swipes in 1912 set a new major league record and he stole 75 more the next year. A career Senator, he became a coach for the team and died of a heart attack during spring training 1953.

SAM RICE, OF (1915-1933)
Rice began his career as a pitcher. His first eight major league appearances were on the mound. He became the Senators' regular right fielder in 1917, when he was 27, and missed all but seven games in 1918 due to military service. Over the next 12 seasons, through his Age-40 season, he was the most durable player in baseball, missing only 53 games. He hit only 34 homers in his career but plenty of singles, doubles, and triples, batting .323/.375/.429 with 351 stolen bases.

GOOSE GOSLIN, OF (1921-1930, 1933, 1938)
His .888 OPS is second only to Killebrew's in franchise history. Like Rice, he was signed as a pitcher, but his bat moved him to the outfield. Defense was never his strong suit, particularly after a self-inflicted arm injury, but he was a consistently excellent hitter, batting .300 or better in seven of his eight full seasons in Washington and .297 in the eighth. He was the team's best hitter every year from 1924 to 1928, hitting .348/.413/.544. His trade back to the club in 1933 helped sparked Washington's last pennant.

TONY OLIVA, OF/DH (1962-1976)
If 50 years ago we had the surgical techniques that we have today, Tony Oliva would be in the Hall of Fame. From his rookie year in 1964 through 1971, he was a perennial All-Star, leading the league in batting three times, doubles four times, and hits five times. He hurt his knee diving for a ball in June 1971, and in the days

before MRIs, arthroscopy, and routine ACL repair, he wasn't the same after that. He had a career .874 OPS up to the injury, .732 over the last 539 games of his career, almost all as a DH.

KIRBY PUCKETT, OF (1984-1985)

The Twins had an unusual number of likeable stars, none more than Puckett. You-know-you're-a-Minnesotan-if line from the 1990s: You have at least one child or pet named Kirby. He hit no home runs his first year in the majors but 20-plus in six other seasons, five times collecting 200 or more hits. He's remembered for single-handedly winning Game Six of the 1991 World Series with his glove and his bat. Glaucoma cut his career short and his final years weren't good ones but his star shone brightly during ten straight All-Star years.

PITCHERS

WALTER JOHNSON, RHP (1907-1927)

Johnson is the franchise record-holder in just about everything, most notably a 417-279 record, 3,509 strikeouts, and a 2.17 career ERA that, even for the Deadball Era, was 47 percent better than average. Known for his fastball, he led the American League in strikeouts an incredible 12 times. He was MVP twice, and in 1913 was 36-7 with a 1.14 ERA in 346 innings, leading the league with 11 shutouts. He even won the seventh game of Washington's only World Series victory in 1924. Johnson was in the inaugural Hall of Fame class and his record of 110 career shutouts looks safe for all time.

FIRPO MARBERRY, RHP (1923-1932, 1936)

There have always been relief pitchers, but Fred Marberry was the first with a role resembling that of closers a half-century later. Between 1924 and 1932 he led the league in games pitched five times, games finished four times, and (retroactively) save six times. He set a record with 15 saves in 1924 and broke it twice in the next two years with his 22 saves in 1926 standing for 23 seasons. He started 133 times for the Senators, relieved 337, and had a 3.59 ERA for the club. He had a .643 winning percentage as a starter, a 3.35 career ERA as a reliever.

DUTCH LEONARD, RHP (1938-1946)

Like Johan Santana, Leonard was a Rule 5 draftee. A knuckleballer, he had a promising start with the Dodgers at 24, but arm problems ensued. He was 29 when he made his first start for Washington, a shutout. Two weeks later, he faced Cleveland's Bob Feller, who shut out the Senators for ten innings, but Leonard shut out the Indians for 13 and won the game, cementing his spot in the rotation. In nine years he went 118-101 with a solid 3.27 ERA for noncompetitive Senators clubs (only two winning seasons in his tenure), topping 210 innings pitched seven times.

CAMILO PASCUAL, RHP (1954-1966)

The 1950s/60s Senators/Twins signed several players from Cuba including Oliva and Pascual. Pascual joined the Senators in 1954, when he was just 20. After initial struggles, he eventually found his bearings and was one of the most dependable pitchers in the league, going 117-81 with a 3.08 ERA from 1958 to 1965. He led the league in complete games, shutouts, and strikeouts three times each. Like Blyleven, his curveball is regarded as one of the best in history.

JIM KAAT, LHP (1959-1973)

Kaat is second to Johnson in franchise history for wins, innings, and starts. The tall lefty averaged over 242 innings pitched per year from 1961 to 1971, maintaining a 3.26 ERA that was 13 percent better than average adjusted for hitter-friendly Metropolitan Stadium. He was an excellent athlete who won 10 straight Gold Gloves in Minnesota and even hit 13 home runs before the DH took the bat out of his hands. Another in the Twins' long line of control pitchers, Kaat walked just 2.2 batters per nine over the course of his 25-season career.

JIM PERRY, RHP (1963-1972)

Gaylord's big brother came to the Twins via a trade with Cleveland. He went 128-90 with a 3.15 ERA in ten Twins seasons. He was a swingman during his first years in Minnesota but when former teammate Billy Martin became manager in 1969, he moved Perry to the rotation. He was a workhorse during the team's back-to-back division championships in 1969 and 1970, going 44-18 with a 2.93 ERA over 540 1/3 innings, winning the 1970 Cy Young Award.

BERT BLYLEVEN, RHP (1970-1976, 1985-1988)

He was a young phenom with a big curveball in his first stint with the club, starting his first game at 19 and compiling a 99-89 record with an outstanding 2.80 for a string of .500-level Twins teams. He returned as a crafty veteran, helping the 1987 Twins win the franchise's first World Series with a 3-1 record in four postseason starts. A prankster during his playing career with a hot-and-cold relationship with fans, he's developed a loyal following as the team's TV color announcer since 1996.

FRANK VIOLA, LHP (1982-1989)

The lefty's first two seasons in Minnesota were forgettable—11-25, 5.38 ERA—but over his next five full seasons, from 1984 to 1988, he was magnificent, going 93-56 with a 3.46 ERA. He pitched 210 or more innings six straight years. He was MVP of the 1987 World Series, winning Game Seven on three days' rest, and followed that with a 24-7, 2.64 ERA, Cy Young Award-winning 1988. Despite his relatively short stay with the club, he ranks third in innings and second in both starts and wins among Senators/Twins lefties.

BRAD RADKE, RHP (1995-2006)

The righty compiled a 4.22 career ERA, all in Minnesota, which, adjusted for the Steroids Era in which he pitched, was 13 percent better than average. He was the staff workhorse beginning in his rookie year, starting 31 or more games nine times. His last season, with his shoulder failing him, he relied on painkillers and cortisone to last through a final season as the team came from a game back of Detroit with four to play to win the AL Central in 2006. An extraordinary control pitcher, he walked an average of 1.6 batters per nine. Nolan Ryan walked 204 batters in 1977 alone; Radke walked 445 in his entire career.

JOHAN SANTANA, LHP (2000-2007)

The Rule 5 draft has had a few iterations, but under current rules, Santana stands out as the best pick ever. Mired in the Astros' farm system, Florida selected him in the 1999 Rule 5 draft and immediately traded him to the Twins. All he did for Minnesota was win two Cy Young Awards (and deserved a third), leading the league in ERA twice and strikeouts three times. Between 2003 and 2007, when teams were scoring five runs per game, he had a 2.92 ERA.

A Taxonomy of 2020 Abnormalities

by Rob Mains

I'm going to start this with a trivia question. Trust me, it's relevant. Don't bother skipping to the end of the article to find the answer, it's not there.

Only five players have appeared in 140 or more games for 16 straight seasons. Who are they?

It's a trivia question starting off an essay, so you know how this works: Whatever you guessed, you're wrong. It's okay. As someone who purchased this book, chances are good that you're an educated baseball fan. But the circumstances behind 2020 force us to abandon, or at least seriously question, some of our favorite patterns and crutches for evaluating the game we love.

We just completed what was undoubtedly the strangest season in MLB history. No fans, geographically limited schedule, universal DH, seven-inning twin bills, runners on second in extra innings, a 16-team postseason, a club playing at a Triple-A stadium. Some of these changes will likely persist (sorry), but we've never had so many tweaks dumped on us all at once, at least not since they figured out how many balls were in a walk.

And the biggest, of course, was the 60-game season. The 19th century was dotted with teams that went bankrupt before the season ended, but the lone season with only 60 scheduled games was 1877. That year there were only six teams, the league rostered a total of 77 players (just 16 more than the 2020 Marlins), and batters called for pitches to be thrown high or low by the pitcher, who was 50 feet away. We can say the 2020 season was easily the shortest ever for recognizable baseball.

As such, it'll stand out. Few abbreviated seasons do. Just about everybody reading this knows the 1994 season ended after Seattle's Randy Johnson struck out Oakland's Ernie Young for the last out of the Mariners-A's game on August 11. The ensuing player strike wiped out the rest of the season and the postseason. Teams played only 112-117 games that year.

And many of you know that a strike in the middle of the 1981 season split the season in two, resulting in the only Division Series until 1995. Teams played only 103-111 games that year, the shortest regular season since 1885.

Those two seasons are memorable. So when we see that nobody drove in 100 runs in 1981, or that Greg Maddux was the only pitcher with 180 or more innings pitched in 1994, we think, "Of course. Strike year."

But we don't remember other short years. You might not recall that the 1994 strike spilled into the next year, chopping 18 games off the 1995 schedule. You might've read that the 1918 season, played during the last pandemic, ended after Labor Day due to the government's World War I "work or fight" order. A strike erased the first week and a half of the 1972 season, but that year's best known as the last time pitchers batted in the American League.

The point is, while we don't remember small changes to the schedule, we remember the big ones. The 1981 mid-season strike. The 1994 season- and Series-ending strike. And, of course, the pandemic-shortened 2020 season. We won't need a reminder why Marcell Ozuna's 18 homers were the fewest to lead the National League in a century. (Literally; Cy Williams led with 15 in 1920.)

Now, about that trivia question. The five players are Hank Aaron, Brooks Robinson, Pete Rose, Ichiro Suzuki, and Johnny Damon. The one nobody gets, of course, is Damon, and a lot of people miss Ichiro, whose last season of 140-plus games came garbed in the red-orange and ocean blue of Miami when he was 42. That's half of what makes it a good question. The other half is the two guys whom many think made the list but didn't. Lou Gehrig? His streak started in the Yankees' 42nd game of the 1925 season and lasted only 13 seasons after that. And everybody assumes Cal Ripken Jr. did it, having played 2,632 straight games over 17 seasons. But one of those 17 seasons was 1994, when the Orioles played only 112 games.

My point? *I just told you* everybody remembers the 1994 strike year, but everybody forgets it fell in the middle of Ripken's streak, separating the first twelve years from the last four. Just because we recall something doesn't mean it's always at the front of our minds.

Nobody is going to forget 2020, and baseball is obviously not the main reason. But there will come a time in the future when you're looking at a player's or a team's record, and there will be baffling numbers there for 2020, and you'll think, "I wonder what happened." (Not to mention the missing line for minor league players.) Just like you forgot that the 1994 strike limited Ripken to 112 games.

Try not to forget it, though. The 2020 season resulted in weird statistical results for several reasons.

There were only 60 games.
I know, duh. But that had impacts beyond counting stats like Ozuna's home run total or Yu Darvish and Shane Bieber leading the majors with eight wins. (I know, pitcher wins, but still.)

The 162-game season is the longest among major North American sports, and that duration gives us a gift. Over the course of a long season, small variations tend to even out. A player who has a ten-game hot streak will probably have a ten-game cold streak. A team that starts the year losing a bunch of close games will probably win a bunch of them. We get regression to the mean. Statistics stabilize.

Consider flipping a coin. Over the long run, we expect it to come up heads about half the time. But the fewer flips, the more variation there'll be. If you flip a coin six times, probability theory tells us you'll get at least two-third heads about 34 percent of the time. Flip it 30 times, your chance of two-thirds heads drops to five percent.

Or, relevant to this case, if you flip a coin 60 times, your chance of getting at least 36 heads—that's 60 percent—is 7.75 percent. Expand the coin-flipping to 162 times, and the chance of getting 60 percent heads drops to 0.73 percent.

In other words, the odds of an outcome that's 20 percent better (or worse) than expected is *more than ten times higher* when you flip your coin 60 times than when you do it 162 times. Call it small sample size, call lack of mean reversion, or call it luck not evening out, 162 is a lot more predictive than 60. You get much more variation over 60 games than over 162. Bieber's 1.63 ERA and 0.87 FIP aren't something we'd see over a full season, and neither is Javier Baéz's .203/.238/.360.

Some players' lines in 2020 look normal. Brian Anderson had an .811 OPS in 2019 and an .810 OPS in 2020. (He probably would have gotten that last point if he'd been given enough time.) But there are many like Bieber and Baéz, some of them from young players still establishing their talent levels. The answer to the question, "What went right or wrong for that guy in 2020?" is most likely "Nothing, it was just a 2020 thing."

Preseason training was abbreviated for hitters.

Every year, spring training drags. Players get tired of it, fans get tired of it, and you sure can tell sportswriters get tired of it. Yes, something to get everyone into shape is necessary, but does it really have to drag on for over a month? Can't we shorten it?

The 2020 season answered in the negative, at least for hitters. Warren Spahn is credited with saying that hitting is timing and pitching is upsetting timing. It appears nobody had his timing down after the abbreviated July summer camp. Through August 9—18 games into the season—MLB batters were hitting .230/.311/.395 with a .275 BABIP. That BABIP, had it held, would have been the lowest since 1968, the Year of the Pitcher. In recent years it's hovered around .300.

It didn't hold. Play returned to more normal levels the rest of the year: .249/.325/.425 with a .297 BABIP starting August 10. But batters whose play concentrated in those first two weeks wound up with ugly lines. Andrew

Benintendi went on the injured list with a season-ending rib cage strain on August 11. His final line: .103/.314/.128 in 14 games. Franchy Cordero went on the IL with a hamate bone fracture on August 9 and a .154/.185/.231 line. Even though he came back strong in a late September return, it was too late to repair his full-season numbers.

Preseason training was abbreviated for pitchers.

Every year, spring training drags. Players get tired of it, fans get tired of it ... wait, I already said that. But the abbreviated preseason was tough on pitchers, too. As noted, they had the upper hand coming out of the gate. But then they lost that hand. And then their arms, too.

The 2020 season was spread over 67 days. During those 67 days, 237 pitchers hit the Injured List, compared to 135 in the first 67 days of 2019. A lot of those IL stints, though, were COVID-19-related. Still, over the first 67 days of the 2019 season, there were 72 pitchers on the IL with arm injuries. That figure jumped to 110 in 2020, a 53 percent increase.

There are a number of factors contributing to pitcher arm injuries, ranging from usage to velocity, but it appears that attenuated preseason training played a role. A lot of pitchers had super-short seasons due to arm woes. Corey Kluber, Roberto Osuna, and Shohei Ohtani combined for seven innings, none after August 8. All suffered arm injuries. We'll never know whether they'd have fared better with a longer preseason, but we can guess how they probably feel.

Everybody played.

Rosters were set to expand from 25 to 26 in 2020, so even if we'd had a normal season, we'd have likely seen 2019's record of 1,410 players on MLB rosters broken. But due to the pandemic, rosters started the year at 30 and were cut to only 28. Add multiple COVID-19 absences and the revolving door caused by poor starts by hitters and a rash of pitcher arm injuries, and 1,289 players appeared in MLB games in 2020. The comparable figure over the first 67 days of the 2019 season was 1,109. That 16 percent increase works out to an average of six more players per team in 2020 compared to a similar slice of 2019. A future look back at 2020 rosters will include a lot of unfamiliar names.

Plus became a minus.

In advanced metrics, we adjust batter and pitcher performance for park and league/era variations. A plus sign appended to the end of a measure means that it's adjusted for park and league. It's scaled to an average of 100, with higher figures above average and lower figures below average. (Similarly, a metric with a minus is also park- and league-adjusted and scaled to 100, with lower values better.) Here at BP, our advanced measure of offensive performance is DRC+. Baseball-Reference has OPS+ and FanGraphs has wRC+.

Using park and league adjustments, we can compare Dante Bichette's 1995 Steroid Era season at pre-humidor Coors Field (.340/.364/.620, 40 homers, 128 RBI, MVP runner-up) with Jim Wynn's 1968 Year of the Pitcher season at the cavernous Astrodome (.269/.376/.474, 26 homers, 67 RBI, no MVP votes). It's not close. DRC+, OPS+, and wRC+ all give the nod to Wynn, handily. This is a useful tool. As my Baseball Prospectus colleague Patrick Dubuque tweeted last fall, "Please note that when I ask how you are, I am already adjusting for era."

The 2020 season messes up plus (and minus) stats for two reasons. First, the park adjustment was based on only 30 home games instead of the usual 81. Everything noted above regarding the short season applies, literally doubly, to park effect calculations. DRC+ uses a single-season park factor. OPS+ uses a three-year average and wRC+ five years. The figure for 2020 is suspect.

Second, OPS+ and wRC+ adjust for league: American and National. (DRC+ adjusts for opponent, regardless of league.) While there were two leagues in 2020, they were an artificial construct. To reduce travel, teams played opponents geographically, not based on league. There weren't two leagues, American and National. There were three, Western, Central, and Eastern.

That makes a difference because teams in the same league played in different run-scoring environments. AL teams scored 4.58 runs per game, NL teams 4.71. That's a small difference. But teams in the East scored 0.21 more runs per game (4.95) than teams in the West (4.74), and they both scored a lot more than Central teams (4.25). Adjusting for league misses that difference, so this book will be safe in that regard, but other sources may be distorted somewhat.

Not every game was a "game."
In 2020, the rising tide of strikeouts was finally stemmed. Strikeouts per team per game fell from 8.8 in 2019 to 8.7 in 2020. That marked the first decline after 14 straight annual increases.

In 2020, the rising tide of strikeouts rose higher. Batters struck out in 23.4 percent of plate appearances compared to 23.0 percent in 2019. That marked the 15th straight annual increase.

Both are true statements.

Because of two rule changes—seven-inning doubleheaders and runners on second in extra innings—games in 2020 were unprecedented in their brevity. There were 37.0 plate appearances per game in 2020. The only years with fewer were 1904 and 1906-1909. The average game in 2020 entailed 8.61 innings pitched, the fewest since 1899.

So when you see any per-game stats for 2020, you need to increase them by 3 or 4 percent to get them on equal footing with recent years.

Minnesota Twins 2021

Or, better, just ignore them. Last year happened. There were major league games contested between major league teams. But when you're looking at those physical or electronic baseball cards, when you're weaving narratives over why this young player's inevitable rise to stardom fell apart or why that old veteran rekindled his magic, don't linger on the 2020 line. It was just too weird.

Thanks to Lucas Apostoleris for research assistance.

—Rob Mains is an author of Baseball Prospectus.

Tranches of WAR

by Russell A. Carleton

We ask "replacement level" to be a lot of things. Sometimes contradictory things. Sometimes I wonder if we know what it even means anymore. The original idea was that it represented the level of production that a team could expect to get from "freely available talent", including bench players, minor leaguers, and waiver wire pickups. It created a common benchmark to compare everyone to, and for that reason, it represented an advancement well beyond what was available at the time. In fact, it created a language and a framework for evaluating players that was not just better but *entirely* different than what came before it.

But then we started mumbling in that language. The idea behind "wins above replacement" was one part sci-fi episode and one part mathematical exercise. Imagine that a player had disappeared before the season and suddenly, in an alternate timeline, his team would have had to replace him. The distance between him and that replacement line was his value. We need to talk about that alternate timeline.

Without getting too into 2:00 am "deep conversations" with extensive navel-gazing, it's worth thinking about why one player might not be playing, while another might.

- A player might not be playing because he has a short-term injury or his manager believes that he needs a day off.
- A player might not be playing because he has a longer-term injury that requires him to be on the injured list.

There's a difference here between these two situations. In particular, the first one generally *doesn't* involve a compensatory roster move, while the second one does. It's possible, though not guaranteed, that the person who will be replacing the injured/resting player would be the same in either case. That matters. Teams generally carry a spare part for all eight position players on the diamond, although in the era of a four-player bench, those spare parts usually are the backup plan for more than one spot.

Minnesota Twins 2021

A couple of years ago, I posed a hypothetical question. Suppose that a team had two players in its system fighting for a fourth outfielder spot. One of them was a league average hitter, but would be worth 20 runs below average if allowed to play center field for a full season. One of them was a perfectly average fielder, but would be 15 runs below average as a hitter, if allowed to play an entire season. Which of the two should the team roster? It's tempting to say the second one, as overall, he is the better player. That misses the point. A league average hitter on the bench isn't just a potential replacement for an injured outfielder. He might also pinch hit for the light-hitting shortstop in a key spot. You keep the average hitter on the roster, even though he isn't a hand-in-glove fit for one specific place on the field, because being a bench player is a different job description than being a long-term fill-in for someone. If you find yourself in need of a longer-term fill-in, you can bring the other guy up from AAA.

When we're determining the value of an everyday player though, if he had disappeared before the season and a team would have had to replace his production, they likely would have done it with a player who was a long-term fill-in type because they would have had to replace a guy who played everyday. Maybe that's the same guy that they would have rostered on their bench anyway, but we don't know. It gets to the query of what we hope to accomplish with WAR. Are we looking for an accurate modeling of reality or are we looking for a common baseline to compare everyone to? Both have their uses, but they are somewhat different questions.

Let's talk about another dichotomy.

- A player might not be playing because he isn't very good and is a bench-level player.
- A player might not be playing because there is another player on the team who has a situational advantage that makes him the better choice today. The classic case of this is a handedness platoon. On another day, he might be a better choice.

When we think about player usage, I think we're still stuck in the model that there are starters and there are scrubs. We have plenty of words for bench players or reserves or backups or utility guys. We do still have the word "platoon" in our collective vocabulary, but in the age of short benches, it's hard to construct one. It's always been hard to construct them. You have to find two players who hit with different hands, have skill sets that complement each other, and probably play the same position. In the era of the short bench, one of them had probably better double as a utility player in some way. Baseball has a two-tiered language geared toward the idea of regulars and reserves. The fact that it was so easy for me to find plenty of synonyms for "a player whose primary function is to come into a game to replace a regular player if he is injured or resting" should tell you something.

I'm always one to look for "unspoken words" in baseball. What is it called when someone is both half of a platoon and the utility infielder? That guy exists sometimes, but he reveals himself in that role—usually by accident. We don't have a word for that, and whenever I find myself saying "we don't have a word for that", I look for new opportunities. What do you call it, further, when the job of being the utility infielder is decentralized across the whole infield with occasional contributions from the left fielder? It's not even a "super-utility" player. What happens when you build your entire roster around the idea that everyone will be expected to be a triple major?

⚾ ⚾ ⚾

I think someone else beat me to this one, and on a grand scale. Platoons work because we know that hitters of the opposite hand to the pitcher get better results than hitters of the same hand, usually to the tune of about 20 points of OBP. If you want to express that in runs, it usually comes out to somewhere around 10 to 12 runs of linear weights value prorated across 650 PA. But hang on a second, now let's say that we have two players who might start today, both of roughly equal merit with the bat. One has a handedness advantage, but is the worse fielder of the two. In that case, as long as his "over the course of a season" projection as a fielder at whatever position you want to slot him into is less than a 10-run drop from the guy he might replace, then he's a better option today.

We're not used to thinking of utility players as bat-first options, who would play below-average defense at three different infield positions. That guy might hook on as a 2B/3B/LF type (Howie Kendrick, come on down!) but teams usually think to themselves that they need as their utility infielder someone who "can handle" shortstop, the toughest of the infield spots to play. If someone can do that *and* hit well, he's probably already starting somewhere, so he's not available as a utility infielder. It's easier for those glove guys to find a job. In a world where the replacement for a shortstop *has to be* the designated utility infielder, that makes sense.

But as we talked about last week, we're living in a different world. The rate at which a replacement for a regular starter turns out to be *another starter* shifting over to cover has gone way up over the last five years. There was always some of it in the game, but this has been a supernova of switcheroos. Now if your second baseman is capable of playing a decent shortstop, that 2B/3B/LF guy can swap in. He's not actually playing shortstop, and maybe the defense suffers from the switch, but if he's got enough of a bat, he might outhit those extra fielding miscues. And in doing so, he is effectively your backup shortstop.

Somewhere along the lines, teams got hip to the idea of multi-positional play from their regulars. I've written before about how you can't just put a player, however athletic, into a new position and expect much at first. The data tell us that. Eventually, players can learn to be multi-positionalists, but it takes time, roughly on the order of two months, before they're OK. But there's a hidden message in there. If you give a player some reps at a new spot, he's a reasonably gifted athlete and somewhat smart and willing to learn, he could probably pick it up enough to get to "good enough," and it doesn't take forever. You just have to be purposeful about it. Maybe you get to the point where you can start to say "he's still below average but we could move him there and get another bat into the lineup, and it's a net win."

Teams have started to build those extra lessons into their player development program. It used to be seen as a mark of weakness to be relegated to "utility player" because that meant that you were a bench player (all those synonyms above come with a side of stigma). Now, it's a way of building a team. If you get a few reps in the minors (where it doesn't count) at a spot, you'll have at least played the spot at game speed before. There are limits to how far you can push that. A slow-footed "he's out in left field because we don't have the DH" guy is never going to play short, but maybe your third baseman can try second base and not look like a total moose out there.

⚾   ⚾   ⚾

Back to WAR. I'd argue that the world of starters and scrubs is slowly disintegrating, for good cause. In the event that a regular starter really does go down with an injury–ostensibly, the alternate universe scenario that WAR is attempting to model–it makes the team a little more resilient to replacing him. And the good news is that you're more likely to be able to replace him with the best of the bench bunch, rather than the third-best guy, because the best guy doesn't have to be an exact positional match for the guy who got hurt. And that's what the manager would want to do. He'd want to replace that long-term production, not with an amalgam of everyone else who played that position, but with the best guy available from his reserves.

Now this is still WAR. We still want to retain the principle that we should be measuring a player, and not his teammates. We need some sort of common baseline, and despite what I just said, we'll still need some sort of amalgam. To construct that, I give to you the idea of the tranche. The word, if you've not heard it before, refers to a piece of a whole that is somehow segmented off. It's often used in finance to talk about layers of a financial instrument.

Here, I want you to consider that there are 30 starters at each of the seven non-battery positions (catchers should have their own WAR, since only a catcher can replace a catcher). We can identify them by playing time, and we can futz around with the definition a little bit if we need to. Next, among those who aren't in that starting pool, we identify the top tranche of the 30 best bench players, which I would again identify by playing time, and then the second and third and fourth and so on. If a player were to disappear, his manager would probably want to take a guy from that top tranche of the bench to replace him. In a world where even the starters can slide around the field, that becomes more feasible.

We can take a look at that top tranche and say "How many of them showed that they are able to play (first, second, etc.)?" and therefore could have directly substituted for the starter? How many of them could have been a direct substitute for our injured player? We don't know whether one of them would be on *a specific* team, but we can say that 40 percent of the time, a manager would have been able to draw from tranche 1 in filling the role, and 35 percent from tranche 2. But on tranche 1, we can also look at how many of those players played a position that could have then shifted and covered for that spot. We'd need some eligibility criteria for all of this (probably a minimum number of games played) but it would just be a matter of multiplication. Shortstop would be harder to fill, and managers would probably be dipping a little further down in the talent pool, and so replacement level would be lower, as it is now.

Doing some quick analysis, I found that the difference in just batting linear weights (haven't even gotten into running or fielding) between tranche 1 and tranche 2 in 2019 was about 6.5 runs, prorated across 650 PA. Between tranche 1 and tranche 3, it's 10.8 runs. The ability to shift those plate appearances up the ladder has some real value.

This part is important. We can also give credit to starters for the positions that they showed an ability to play, even if they didn't play them (this is the guy fully capable of playing center, but who's in a corner because the team already has a good center fielder) because he allows a team to carry a player who hits like a left fielder to functionally be the team's backup center fielder. He facilitates that movement upward among the tranches. We can start to appreciate the difference between a left fielder who would never be able to hack it in center (and the compensatory move that his team would have to make) and the left fielder who could do it, but just didn't have to very often.

Past that, you can continue to use whatever hitting and fielding and running metrics you like to determine a player's value, but when we get down to constructing that baseline, I'd argue we need a better conceptual and mathematical framework. It's going to require some more #GoryMath than we're used to, but I'd argue it's a better conceptualization of the way that MLB actually plays the game in 2020. If…y'know…MLB plays in 2020. If WAR is going to be our flagship statistic among the *acronymati*, then we need to acknowledge that it contains some old and starting-to-be-out-of-date assumptions about the game. We may need to tinker with it. Here's my idea for how.

—*Russell A. Carleton is an author of Baseball Prospectus.*

Secondhand Sport

by Patrick Dubuque

Back before time stopped, I liked to go to thrift stores. Now that I'm older, I rarely ever buy anything—I don't need much in my life, now—but I still enjoy the old familiar circuit: check to see if there are baseball cards to write about, look for board or card games to play with the kids, scan for random ironic jerseys, hit the book section. It takes ten, maybe fifteen minutes. Thrift stores are the antithesis of modern online shopping, because you don't know what they have, and you don't even really know what you want. It's junk, literal junk, stuff other people thought was worthless. That's what makes it great.

In an idealized economy, thrift stores shouldn't exist. Everybody has a living wage, and every product has a durability that exactly matches its desired life; nothing should need to be given away, no one should need to be given to. But then, thrift stores shouldn't work on a customer experience level, either. You wouldn't think an ethos of "let's make everything disorganized and hard to find" would lead to customer satisfaction, but low-budget retailers like TJ Maxx and Ross thrive on this model. People like bargain hunting as much for the hunting as the bargain; it's part of the experience, spending time as if it's a wager. There's a thrill, occasionally, in inefficiency.

In sports, the modern overuse of the word "inefficiency" is a condemnation: It insinuates that there is *an* efficiency, a correct way to be found, and that all other ways are wrong ways. It's prevalent in baseball but hardly contained to it; the lifehack, the Silicon Valley disruption are other examples of productivity creep in our daily lives. Their modern success makes plenty of sense. Maximization of resources, after all, is its own puzzle, and an industry of European board games is founded upon it. It's fun to take a system and optimize it, unravel it like a sudoku puzzle. If there's only one kind of genius, after all, there's no way anyone can fail to appreciate it.

Baseball has been hacking away at these perceived inefficiencies since its inception: platoons, bullpens, farm systems were all installed to extract more out of the tools at hand. But it's been a particular badge of the sabermetric movement, from Ken Phelps and his All-Star Team to Ricardo Rincon and the darlings of *Moneyball*. It's business, but it's also an ethos: the idea that there's treasure among the trash, something we all failed to appreciate until someone brought it to light.

It's the myth that made Sidd Finch so enticing, that fuels so many "best shape" narratives and new pitch promises. We all, athletes and unathletic sportswriters, want to believe that there's genius trapped inside us, and that it's just a matter of puzzling out the combination to unlock it. That our art, our style is the next inefficiency, waiting for our own Billy Beane. It's why we root for underdogs, and why we're excited for the Mike Tauchmans and the Eurubiel Durazos, champions of skin-deep mediocrity.

Except we aren't anymore, really. The days of "Free X" have descended beyond the ring of irony and into obscurity. There are still Xs to be freed, or at least one X, duplicated endlessly: Mike Ford, Luke Voit, Max Muncy. The undervalued one-dimensional slugger demonstrated how the game hasn't quite culturally caught up to its logical extreme. But for those who don't fit the rather spacious mold, times are grimmer. As Rob Arthur revealed several months ago, there's been a marked increase in the number of sub-replacement relievers. It's the outcome of a greater number of teams forced to play out games without the talent to win them, but it's also emblematic of the modern tendency of teams to dispose of their disposable assets, burning through cost-controlled arms the way that man chopped down forests in *The Lorax*. Stuff just isn't built to outlive their original owners anymore.

It's unsurprising, given how well-mined the market for inefficiencies has been of late. The disciples of the early analytics departments, and the disciples of those, have proliferated the league, with only a few backwater holdouts. The league has grown smarter, but every team has learned the same lesson. In fact, the phenomenon creates a peculiar kind of feedback loop: As teams value a specific subset of players or skills, prospective athletes learn to increase their own marketability by conforming themselves to the demands of their prospective employers.

And that's tragic, in the way that the extinction of animals is tragic; a certain amount of biodiversity in baseball has been lost. Shortstops hit like outfielders. Pitchers don't hit at all. Only the catchers remain idiosyncratic, thanks to the defensive demands of their position; eventually they too will be required to produce like everyone else, or they'll meet the fate of their battery mates. A perfect economy requires perfect production.

I mentioned earlier that more and more, I leave thrift stores empty-handed. It is true that I am more discerning than in the past; my bookshelves are full, and there are more streaming films than I will ever be able to watch. But there are other factors at play.

Thrift stores are, in a way, the bond markets of retail. When the economy is rough and other retailers are struggling, more people look secondhand for their products. But as recently as last year, publications were noting a reversal of the trend: Companies like Goodwill and Savers were expanding despite a strong economy. Publications credited a heightened sense of environmentalism and a rejection of cutting-edge fashion as drivers behind the increase, though the more likely answer is the modern American economy hasn't showered its favors equally, particularly among the young.

But it is more than just the economy. Baseball and thrift stores share something else in common, evident in our current conversations about re-starting the sport: They live in the gray area between public service and private enterprise. Thrift stores provide affordable necessities to lower-class citizens, and collectibles and fashion for the middle-class. Because of the success of the latter, prices have gone up across the board. Especially in terms of clothing, the middle-class flight from fashion into vintage has instead carried the aftereffects of fashion, including its costs, into a territory where people just want clothes. But there's another factor in the rise of prices, in the form of the internet.

The Goodwills of the world have grown smarter, too, employing the internet to extract full value from their detritus. Ebay, similarly, has lost much of the charm it had as a new frontier around the turn of the century. Everything has a price point now; even individual taste is no match for the algorithm, because anything rare, no matter how niche its market, is a collectible to someone.

The internet has had the same effect on thrift stores that sabermetrics has had on baseball; its equivalent to OBP was the bar scanner. As detailed in Slate, the rise of second-party stores on eBay and Amazon birthed an entire industry of used-good salespeople, armed with PDAs and scanners, buying books for three dollars to sell online for five. The author, Michael Savitz, reports earning $60,000 by working nearly 80 hours a week; he makes it clear that this is not a vocation of his choosing. It's long hours, with no real creativity or individuality, skimming the cream off of a local establishment and flipping it to someone with a little more money on the other side of the country. And once the vocation exists, the obvious question arises: why wait to put the wares out on the shelves? Why allow value to exist at all?

Nothing is ruined. Thrift stores will continue to sell polo shirts and DVDs, and baseball will continue to exist and make or lose money, depending on who you believe. But as we continue to refine our knowledge, we lose something in the conquest for efficiency, a delight born out of the unknown. The problem isn't the efficiency itself; we can't blame the booksellers, or the people sweeping freeways to collect grams of platinum from damaged catalytic converters. The problem is a system that requires this sort of profit-skimming behavior in order to feed families (or, for corporations, maximize shareholder return).

Minnesota Twins 2021

In times like these, with the 2020 season on the brink and the collective bargaining agreement close behind, it can often feel like the current situation is untenable. It can't keep going like this, even if we don't know what to do about it. But as with thrift stores, there's an equally irresistible feeling that it *has* to keep going, that it would be unimaginable to not have this broken, amazing sport. Both industries exist on an invisible foundation of friction, of chaos and unpredictability, even as both see their foundations buffed down to a perfect, untouchable polish. But if COVID-19 and its financial ramifications do, as some have suggested, make it such that the baseball that returns is fundamentally different than the baseball that came before, perhaps this is the time to lean in, and change the game even more. Fix bunting. Make defense more difficult. Create viable, alternate strategies. Add some chaos back into baseball. It's fun when no one knows quite where things are.

—Patrick Dubuque is an author of Baseball Prospectus.

Steve Dalkowski Dreaming

by Steven Goldman

We dream of being a pitcher, of starring in the major leagues. Depending on your age and your sense of historical perspective, you might imagine yourself as Walter Johnson, throwing harder than anyone else—hitting more batters than anyone else, too, but always feeling bad about it. You could picture yourself as a Tom Seaver or a David Cone, with all the stuff in the world but still being cerebral about it, thinking about so much more than burning 'em in there. There are so many models one could choose: You could be a Lefty Gomez, Jim Bouton, or Bill Lee, skilled, but not taking the whole thing too seriously, or a Lefty Grove, Bob Gibson, or Steve Carlton, powerful but treating each start like a mission to be survived instead of a game to be enjoyed.

Very few would dream of being Steve Dalkowski, the former Baltimore Orioles prospect who died of COVID-19 last week at the age of 80. Yet, there is something just as noble in Dalkowski's negative accomplishments—and accomplishments is what they are—as there is in the precision-engineered pitching of a Greg Maddux. You have to be very good to be that bad. Dalkowski had all of the stuff of the greatest pitchers but none of the command; his story is not one of failing to conquer his limitations, but striving against one of the cruelest hands that fate or genetics or personality can deal us: A desire to achieve great things which is almost but not quite matched by the ability to meet that goal.

As with Johnson, Grove, Bob Feller, and the rest of the hard-throwing pitchers who played before the advent of modern radar guns, we have to take the word of the players and coaches who saw Dalkowski pitch as to his velocity. He was a hard-drinking, maximum-effort pitcher who, if their memories are to be believed, consistently threw over 100 miles per hour. His was the Maltese Fastball, the stuff that dreams are made of. The problem is that velocity without command and control is still a good distance from utility. Dalkowski was the most effective towel you could design for a fish, the sleekest bathing suit intended to be worn by an astronaut, but that doesn't mean he wasn't beautiful: We can appreciate a journey even if it doesn't end at the intended destination.

Whether because of sloppy mechanics he couldn't calm, an inability to understand that a consistent 98 in the strike zone would likely be more effective than a consistent 110 out of it, or all that beer, Dalkowski could never make the adjustments that pitchers like Feller and Nolan Ryan made before him, possibly because he had so far to go: Feller, who never pitched in the minors, came up at 17 and spent three years walking almost seven batters per nine innings before settling in at 3.8 beginning when he was 20. Ryan started out walking over six batters per nine but gradually improved as his long career played out; for him to go from 6.2 walks per nine with the 1966 Greenville Mets to 3.7 with the 1989 Texas Rangers represents a 40 percent reduction. An equivalent improvement by Dalkowski would still have left him walking over 11 batters per nine innings.

Dalkowski was like *The Room* of pitchers, a player so bad he became good again. Cal Ripken, Sr., who both played with and managed Dalkowski, recalled in a 1979 *Sporting News* "where are they now" piece the occasion when the pitcher crossed up his catcher and his fastball, "hit the plate umpire smack in the mask. The mask broke all to pieces and the umpire wound up in the hospital for three days with a concussion. If they ever had a radar gun in those days, I'll bet Dalkowski would have been timed at 110 miles an hour."

Signed by the Orioles out of New Britain High in Connecticut in 1957, Dalkowski was sent to Kingsport in the Appalachian League, where he pitched 62 innings. He allowed only 22 hits in 62 innings, or 3.2 per nine, a number with no equivalent in major league history (though Aroldis Chapman came close in 2014), and also struck out 121 (17.6 per nine) and walked 129 (18.7). He was also charged with 39 wild pitches. That June, one of his fastballs clipped a Dodgers prospect named Bob Beavers and carried away part of his ear. "The first pitch was over the backstop, the second pitch was called a strike, I didn't think it was," Beavers said last year. "The third pitch hit me and knocked me out, so I don't remember much after that. I couldn't get in the sun for a while, and I never did play baseball again." Former minor leaguer Ron Shelton based the *Bull Durham* pitcher Nuke LaLoosh on Dalkowski. And yet, to see him as a figure of fun, an amusing loser, is to misunderstand something unique and strange.

Dalkowski kept on posting some of the strangest lines in baseball history. Pitching for the Stockton Ports of the Class C California League in 1960, he struck out 262 and walked 262 in 170 innings. Yet, he did improve, especially after pitching for Earl Weaver at Elmira in 1962. Weaver had previously had Dalkowski at Aberdeen in 1959, but wasn't ready to grapple with him then. This time he was. "I had grown more and more concerned about players with great physical abilities who could not learn to correct certain basic deficiencies no matter how much you instructed or drilled them," he related in his autobiography, *It's What You Learn After You Know It All That Counts*. He got permission from the Orioles to give all of his players the Stanford-Binet IQ test. "Dalkowski finished in the 1 percentile in his ability to understand facts. Steve, it was said to say, had the ability to do everything but learn." [sic]

IQ tests are problematic diagnostic tools, so take Weaver's estimate of Dalkowski's mental capabilities with a grain of salt. What's important is that even if he got to the right answer by way of the wrong reason, Weaver had learned something valuable. His insight was to stop asking Dalkowski to learn new pitches and just let him get by with the two that he had. Were Dalkowski a prospect today, that would have been a no-brainer: Can't develop a third pitch? The bullpen is right over there, sir. Player development wasn't like that then, but Weaver, temporarily Dalkowski's mentor, could let him work with what he had. According to Weaver, the pitcher responded: "In the final 57 innings he pitched that season Dalkowski gave up 1 earned run, struck out 110 batters, and walked only 11." It's not true—as per the *Elmira Star-Gazette*, as of late July, Dalkowski had walked 71 in 106 innings and finished with 114 in 160 innings, which means Dalkowski's control actually faded at the end of the season rather than improved—but that doesn't mean it didn't happen in some sense, just that it didn't happen that way. Again, it's the journey, not the destination, and his ERA was 3.04 so *something* had gone right.

Also along the way: The next spring, Orioles manager Billy Hitchcock was rooting for Dalkowski to make the team as a long-man—maybe Weaver had gotten through to him. There were things out of Weaver's control, like the universe's twisted sense of humor: that March, Dalkowski's elbow went "twang."

You sometimes read that it was the Orioles' insistence on Dalkowski learning the curve that did him in, but even if they hadn't learned their lesson, the injury was probably just a coincidence: Dalkowski had thrown an incredible number of pitches over the previous few years. Still, it testifies to the dangers of trying to get what you want and risking the loss of what you had. Dalkowski tried to come back, but the 110-mph stuff was gone. A pitcher with no control and no stuff is…a civilian. What followed were years of vagabond living, arrests for drunkenness. There were Alcoholics Anonymous meetings, assistance from baseball alumni associations, but none of it took. From the 1990s until the time of his passing he dwelt in an assisted living facility, suffering from alcohol-related dementia. He'd been a heavy drinker since his teenage years. As with all those pitches per game, there was a price to be paid. You make choices on the journey and some of them are irrevocable. It's like a fairy tale: "Bite of poison apple? Don't mind if I do."

In the aforementioned *Sporting News* profile, Chuck Stevens, the head of the Association of Professional Ballplayers of America, a ballplayer charity, said, "I've got nothing against drinking. I do it myself sometimes. But, I don't condone common drunkenness. We went through lots of heartache and many dollars, but Dalkowski didn't want to help himself and we weren't going to keep him drunk." The journey is *un*like a fairy tale: No one will come along and kiss it better, not if they're busy forming judgments.

In the end, we are left with a sort of philosophical chicken/egg conundrum: Is failing to meet your goals evidence of unfulfilled potential or the lack of it? Isn't what you did by definition what you were capable of doing? Or could you have broken through to something better with the right help, the right lucky break? These are unanswerable questions, and how we try to answer them may say more about us than about the people we're judging.

No pitcher ever has it easy. *All* pitchers must work hard. *All* pitchers must refine their craft. It's almost never just about *stuff*. Dalkowski dreaming is no insult to the great pitchers who made it; from Pete Alexander to Max Scherzer, they have all earned their way up. And yet, if it is true that we can only do as much as we can do, then the journey would be more of an adventure, the ultimate triumph or defeat more noble, if like Dalkowski we lacked 100 percent of the confidence, the command, the self-possession, the commitment, the resistance to making bad decisions that so many great players possess—to be gloriously human. Or, to put it more succinctly, it would be fun to be able to throw as hard as any person ever has. Even if just for a moment, and even if nothing more came of it than that, no one could say you hadn't lived life to the fullest.

—*Steven Goldman is an author of Baseball Prospectus.*

A Reward For A Functioning Society

by Cory Frontin and Craig Goldstein

On July 5, Nationals reliever Sean Doolittle said in the middle of a press conference regarding the restart of Major League Baseball and what would later be known as summer camp, "sports are like the reward of a functioning society." This sentence was amidst a much longer, thoughtful reply about the societal and health conditions under which MLB players were being brought back. It's a very similar sentiment to one Jane McManus used on April 7, when she discussed the White House's meeting with sports commissioners. She said "sports are the effect of a functioning society—not the precursor."

Both versions of the same sentiment spoke to a laudable ideal in the context of a country that was not addressing a rampaging virus, and opting instead to bring sports back for the feeling of normalcy rather than the reality of it. "Priorities," as McManus said.

On Wednesday, the NBA's Milwaukee Bucks conducted a wildcat/political strike, refusing to come out for Game 5 of their playoff series against the Orlando Magic. The Magic refused to accept the forfeit, and shortly thereafter other playoff series were threatened by player strikes. Eventually the league moved to postpone that day's games, folding to players leveraging their united power.

The backdrop against which these actions took place was the shooting by police of Jacob Blake. Blake was shot in the back seven times by police, as he attempted to get into his vehicle. He managed to survive the assault, but is paralyzed from the waist down.

⚾ ⚾ ⚾

The step taken to walk out, first by the Milwaukee Bucks, then subsequently by other NBA, WNBA, and MLB teams, was a step toward upholding the virtue of the sentiment described by McManus and Doolittle. But that sentiment does not align with the broad history of sports in this and other countries, a history that contradicts the core of the idealistic statement.

Sports have been a significant part of American society for most of its existence, expanding in importance and influence in recent years. The idea that society was functioning in a way that was worthy of the reward of sports for most of that time is laughable. Much of America is not functioning and has not functioned for Black people, full stop. The oppressed people at the center of this political act by players, specifically Black players, in concert throughout the NBA and in fits and starts throughout Major League Baseball, have not known a society that functions for them rather than *because* of them.

Politics has been part of the sports landscape since the inception of sport, but for just about as long people have bemoaned its presence. Sports are to be an escape, it is said. An escape from what, though? A functioning society?

No, the presence of sports has never signified a cultural or political system that is on the up and up. Rather, the presence of sports *reflect and reinforce the society that produces them.*

⚾   ⚾   ⚾

The Negro Leagues were born out of societal dysfunction. The need for entirely separate leagues, composed of Black and Latino players barred from the Major Leagues because of racism? That is not a functioning society, and yet there were sports.

Even the integration of players from the Negro Leagues resulted in a transfer of power and wealth from Black-owned businesses and communities and into white ones, mirroring the dysfunction that had bled into every aspect of American society at the time. Japheth Knopp noted in the Spring 2016 Baseball Research Journal:

> *The manner in which integration in baseball—and in American businesses generally—occurred was not the only model which was possible. It was likely not even the best approach available, but rather served the needs of those in already privileged positions who were able to control not only the manner in which desegregation occurred, but the public perception of it as well in order to exploit the situation for financial gain. Indeed, the very word integration may not be the most applicable in this context because what actually transpired was not so much the fair and equitable combination of two subcultures into one equal and more homogenous group, but rather the reluctant allowance—under certain preconditions—for African Americans to be assimilated into white society.*

To understand the value of a movement, though, is not to understand how it is co-opted by ownership, but to know the people it brings together and what they demand. When Jackie Robinson—the player who demarcated the inevitability of the end of the Negro leagues—attended the March on Washington for Jobs and Freedom in 1963, he did so with his family and marched alongside the people. He stood alongside hundreds of thousands to fight for their common civil and labor rights. "The moral arc of the universe is long," many freedom fighters have echoed, "but it bends towards justice." The bend, it is less frequently said, happens when a great mass of people place the moral arc of the universe on their knee and apply force, as Jackie, his family, and thousands of others did that day.

⚾ ⚾ ⚾

Of course, taking the moral arc of the universe down from the mantle and bending it is not without risk. Perhaps the outsized influence of athletes is itself a mark of a dysfunctional society, but, nonetheless, hundreds of athletes woke up on Wednesday morning with the power to bring in millions of dollars in revenues. That very power, as we would come to find out, was matched with the equal and opposite power to *not* bring those revenues. That power, in hands ranging from the Milwaukee Bucks, to Kenny Smith in the *Inside the NBA* Studio, from the unexpected ally, Josh Hader, and his largely white teammates to the notably Black Seattle Mariners, would be exercised for a single demand: the end to state violence against Black people. Not unlike the March itself, it sat at the intersection of the civil rights of Black Americans and bold labor action. The March on Washington stood in the face of a false notion of integration—against an integration of extraction but not one of equality—and proposed something different. Just the same, the acts of solidarity of August 26, 2020 will be remembered in stark defiance of MLB's BLM-branded, but ultimately empty displays on opening weekend.

Bold defiance like this can never be without risk. By choosing to exercise this power, the Milwaukee Bucks took a risk. They risked vitriol and backlash from those they disagreed with. They risked fines or seeing their contracts voided, as a walkout like this is prohibited by their CBA. They risked forfeiting a playoff game, one that, as the No. 1 seed in the playoffs, they'd worked all year to attain. They didn't know how Orlando would respond. It wasn't clear that other teams throughout the league would follow suit in solidarity. And it wasn't known the league would accept these actions and moderately co-opt them by "postponing" games that would have featured no players.

If the league reschedules the games, some of the athletes' risk—their shared sacrifice—will be diminished, in retrospect. But they did not know any of that when they took that risk. And it is often left to athletes to take these risks when others in society won't, especially those of their same socioeconomic status and levels of influence.

It is athletes, specifically BIPOC athletes, that take them, though, because they live with the risk of being something other than white in this country every day. They are no strangers to the realities of police brutality. It seems incongruous then, to say that sports are a reward for a functioning society when we rely on athletes to lead us closer to being a functioning society. Luckily, our beloved athletes, WNBA players first and foremost among them, understand what sports truly are: a pipebender for the moral arc of the universe.

—Craig Goldstein is editor in chief of Baseball Prospectus. Cory Frontin is an author of Baseball Prospectus.

Index of Names

Alcala, Jorge 36
Anderson, Shaun 38
Arraez, Luis 14
Astudillo, Williams 68
Bailey, Homer 81
Balazovic, Jordan 82, 93
Berríos, José 40
Blankenhorn, Travis 69
Buxton, Byron 16
Canterino, Matt 94
Cavaco, Keoni 69, 95
Cave, Jake 18
Celestino, Gilberto 70, 97
Chalmers, Dakota 82
Choi, Hyun-wook 71
Clippard, Tyler 42
Colomé, Alex 44
Cruz, Nelson 20
Dobnak, Randy 46
Donaldson, Josh 72
Duffey, Tyler 48
Duran, Jhoan 83, 92
Garver, Mitch 22
Gonzalez, Marwin 24
Gordon, Nick 73
Hamilton, Ian 84
Happ, J.A. 50
Hill, Rich 52
Javier, Wander 73
Jeffers, Ryan 26, 92
Kepler, Max 28
Kirilloff, Alex 74, 90
Larnach, Trevor 75, 91
Lewis, Royce 76, 89
Lin, Tzu-Wei 77
Maeda, Kenta 54
Odorizzi, Jake 56
Pérez, Hernán 78
Pineda, Michael 58
Polanco, Jorge 30
Raya, Marco 98
Robles, Hansel 60
Rodriguez, Jefry 85
Rogers, Taylor 86
Romo, Sergio 62
Rooker, Brent 79, 96
Sabato, Aaron 80, 95
Sanó, Miguel 32
Simmons, Andrelton 34
Smeltzer, Devin 87
Soularie, Alerick 80, 98
Stashak, Cody 64
Thielbar, Caleb 66
Thorpe, Lewis 88
Urbina, Misael 97
Winder, Josh 97

For the Joy of Keeping Score

THIRTY81 Project is an ongoing graphic design project focused on the ballparks of baseball. Since being established in 2013, scorecards have been a fundemantal part of the effort. Each two-page card is uniquely ballpark-centric — there are 30 variants — and designed with both beginning and veteran scorekeepers in mind. Evolving over the years with suggestions from fans, broadcasters, and official scorers, the sheets are freely available to everyone as printable letter-size PDFs at the project webshop: www.THIRTY81Project.com

Download, Print, Score, Repeat …

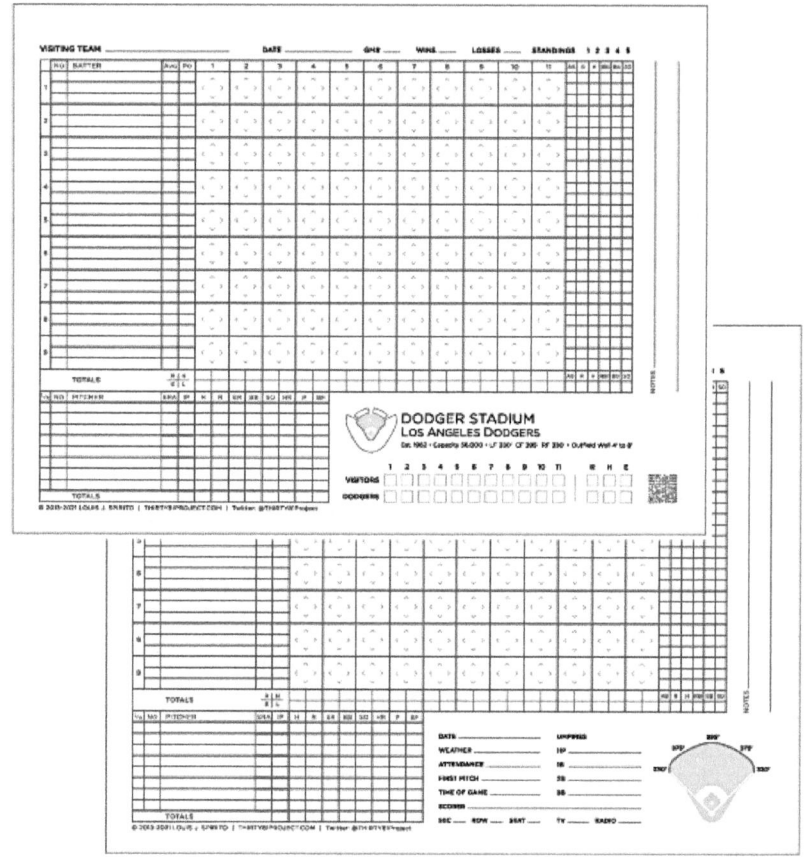